Minding the Body,
Mending the Mind

v

Minding the Body,

Mending the Mind

Joan Borysenko, Ph.D.
with Larry Rothstein

BANTAM BOOKS
TORONTO · NEW YORK · LONDON · SYDNEY · AUCKLAND

To my husband, Myrin—
teacher, learner, lover, and friend.

Contents

Foreword

I had the good fortune to meet Dr. Joan Borysenko during the summer of 1968, when she had just graduated from Bryn Mawr College and had taken the position of research assistant in the same physiologic laboratory at the Harvard Medical School in which I was a Fellow. We worked together on a project studying the effects of environmental stress on the blood pressure of monkeys. The team was ultimately successful in demonstrating not only that we could control blood pressure in these animals through the use of biofeedback-operant conditioning techniques, but that we were able to train the monkeys to induce and reverse high blood pressure. After that summer, Dr. Borysenko started her doctoral studies in another field—cellular biology.

At that same time I was just beginning my studies of Transcendental Meditation. With several other teams over the next decade, I was able to define the physiologic changes of meditation, which led ultimately to the definition of the relaxation response. We also established the value of the relaxation response in the treatment of high blood pressure and other disorders related to stress.

By 1978, Dr. Borysenko was pursuing a career in cancer research in the Department of Anatomy and Cellular Biology at Tufts Medical School, having completed a postdoctoral fellowship in Experimental Pathology. But she had followed the scientific definition of the beneficial physiology of the relaxation response by becoming a practitioner and teacher of meditation and yoga. Dr. Borysenko called me and asked whether it might be possible for her to join our laboratory, then at Boston's Beth Israel Hospital. She explained that she wished to consider a shift in her scientific career in order to achieve more contact with research that was focused on the relaxation response and other mind-body interactions. By chance, our Behavioral Medicine Unit had just received its first National Institutes of Health training grant. Dr. Borysenko became one of the first trainees under this award, and she has been a most valued and trusted colleague since.

In September 1981, Dr. Borysenko and Dr. Ilan Kutz started the Mind/Body Clinic. It was designed to train patients to elicit the relaxation response and, upon that base, to add other nondrug treatments that included nutrition, stretching exercises, and training in the attitudes of stress-hardiness and awareness. Shortly thereafter, Dr. Borysenko became director of the clinic, continuing to integrate traditional, time-honored treatments with those of modern medicine. The Mind/Body Clinic has achieved standards of excellence and therapeutic successes that attract people from throughout the world, both patients for treatment and medical professionals for training. The Mind/Body Clinic is an essential component of the section in Behavioral Medicine.

Minding the Body, Mending the Mind is a highly readable and enjoyable book, presenting the methods of treatment used in the Mind/Body Clinic. Making liberal use of case histories to convey major principles of the clinic, it offers a broad-based integrative approach based on the relaxation response and the other research of our section, combined with the unique warmth and teaching ability of Joan Borysenko. I am confident that now, by virtue of these writings, many more people can be helped.

Herbert Benson, M.D.
Boston
January 1987

Acknowledgments

The process of writing this book stimulated recollections of my own evolution from worrier to warrior—a quip that I attribute to my friend and colleague Ilan Kutz, M.D., who helped found the Mind/Body Clinical Program with Herbert Benson, M.D., and me in September 1981. As I continue my own journey of awakening and growth, new understandings find their way into my work. My patients have often stimulated those understandings, giving inspiration to me and to one another in the sharing of their struggles and victories. I thank them every one.

Many others have helped in the production of this book, either personally or professionally. Perhaps the best way to acknowledge them is in chronological order. My father, Edward Zakon, taught me lessons in love and courage. His own death from cancer and struggle to overcome his fears were a vital force in my life. Fortunately, my mother, Lillian, has a famous sense of humor that kept the rest of us from taking ourselves too seriously. My brother, Alan, ten years my senior, was like a third parent when I was a child and has remained an invaluable source of love and support throughout my life.

Scientific mentors who have passed on knowledge that has served as a foundation for new directions include William Morse, Ph.D., and Jean Paul Revel, Ph.D., who taught me the scientific method, and Morris Karnovsky, M.B., B.Ch., D.Sc., whose incredible searching mind always challenged his students to broaden their perspectives. Herbert Benson has done a great service in elucidating the physiology and clinical usefulness of the relaxation response and in helping to father the field of behavioral medicine. I am indebted to him for the supportive atmosphere he has created for me and others to continue the exploration of mind/body interactions, and for his faith in me and in our program. David McClelland, Ph.D., taught me that scientific theory, combined with the art of astute observation and a respect for intuition, can lead to breakthroughs in understanding.

Many valued colleagues have contributed to my work. Karen Hitchcock, Ph.D., and Murry Blair, Ph.D., were instrumental in helping change the direction of my career from basic laboratory research to clinical practice. Stephen Maurer, M.A., joined the Mind/Body Clinic in 1983. His understanding of meditation and the mind has added substantially to the program, as have his wit and warmth. The chapter on mind traps is adapted from a system that Steve first introduced to me, and many of the stories are also Steve's gifts.

A very special thanks also is due to Jon Kabat-Zinn, Ph.D., founder and director of the Stress Reduction and Relaxation Program at the University of Massachusetts Medical School at Worcester, who inspired us to set up the Mind/Body Clinic and helped us with its format and content in the early days; and to Jane Leserman, Ph.D., who has done wonderful work in evaluating the program and developing self-assessment tools, including the medical symptom checklist in the self-assessment section of this book. My colleague Steven Locke, M.D., has shared his interest and enthusiasm in psychiatry and psychoneuroimmunology. I thank him for his support and for our many stimulating conversations.

Other valued colleagues whose work is directly or indirectly part of my understanding include Catherine Morrison, L.I.C.S.W., Olivia Hoblitzelle, M.A., Eileen Stuart, R.N., M.S., Margaret Caudill, M.D., Ph.D., George Everly, Ph.D., Basil Barr, M.D., Naomi Remen, M.D., Michael Lerner,

Ph.D., Dean Ornish, M.D., Leo Stolbach, M.D., the late John Hoffman, Ph.D., Tom Stewart, M.D., Matthew Budd, M.D., David Eisenberg, M.D., Rick Ingrasci, M.D., Robin Casarjian, M.A., Norman Cousins, Bernie Siegel, M.D., Kenneth Pelletier, Ph.D., Brendan O'Regan of the Institute of Noetic Sciences, and Eileen Rockefeller Growald, whose vision in founding the Institute for the Advancement of Health has promoted public understanding of mind/body interactions and afforded many of the researchers and clinicians in this area with an invaluable forum for interaction.

Thanks to Nancy MacKinnon, Gail Cammarata, Roxanne Daleo, M.A., Janet Romano, Claudia Dorrington, Amy Saltz, Debbie Lee, and Sheila Cusack for their valuable program support. Special thanks to Margaret Ennis for her thorough and professional administrative support of the program, her warm and caring interaction with our patients, and the love that she devotes to all of us. Thanks also to the administrative staff of Boston's Beth Israel Hospital, which provided the home for the Mind/Body Clinic to grow up in. Thanks also to our new home, the New England Deaconess Hospital, whose commitment to the care of the whole patient interested them in developing a strong section in behavioral medicine.

Thanks are also due to psychological and spiritual mentors. Harriett Mann, Ed.D., was a treasure in helping me and Myrin understand and accept ourselves and each other. The Reverend Chris Williamson performed a similar function, reacquainting me with God in the process. The reacquaintance has been continued through the teachings of the late Swami Muktananda and his successor Swami Chidvilasananda in the tradition of Siddha Yoga.

Many people have been critical to the book project itself. Larry Rothstein called one Monday morning inviting me to write a book about executive stress. I accepted. It soon became clear to his patient and practiced listening that my heart really lay in writing a book about the Mind/Body Program. I am extremely grateful for his setting the process into motion and for being its caring shepherd from its inception. He and Ken Rivard did a splendid job in helping me put together a book proposal, a task as daunting as my first National Institutes of Health grant proposal. My agent, Helen Rees, was unfailingly supportive, both to me and to the project. My editor at Addison-Wesley, William Patrick, has been much more than an editor. His enthusiasm has been a guiding light and his touch present in every aspect of the project. His support, together with the continuing guidance of Larry Rothstein, made it possible to enjoy an experience that might have been a stressful one. Lori Snell, Copenhaver Cumpston, Carolyn Savarese, Diane Hovenesian, and George Gibson of Addison-Wesley have made all aspects of the book process—from production through public relations—a complete delight. Thank you all. Peter Rosenblatt, a second-year medical student, did a fine job of illustrating the stretches from photos he shot of me on the patio one drizzly summer's morning.

Now I know why authors always end by lauding the special virtues of their family's patience. Adding a book to a schedule that is already overflowing has meant that my sons, Justin and Andrei, have become very good cooks. Their wives will thank me someday. My stepdaughter, Natalia, has also been gracious in putting up with my schedule, as has my mother, Lillian. My husband, Myrin, has been colleague, consultant, troubleshooter, editor, therapist, chief cook, and bottle washer. His love, affection, and support have really made this project a reality.

Introduction

When I was twenty-four I was working on my doctoral dissertation at the Harvard Medical School, investigating the way cells maintain their attachment to one another. I was living on coffee and cigarettes, broke and tired, trying to cope with a troubled marriage and an infant son for whom I had far too little time. I was a relentless perfectionist, trying to control and succeed at everything.

I was also a physical wreck. Troubled by migraines all my life, I found in college that the intense competition had added crippling stomach pains and vomiting to my list of psychosomatic illnesses. As a graduate student, I also came down with severe bronchitis four times in two years and had to study for my doctoral exams while my head spun in a fever. If this weren't enough, I also developed the high blood pressure that ran in my family.

My marriage fell apart during this year. I was now a single parent plagued with fainting and crippled by abdominal pains that were diagnosed as spastic colon. I was given antispasmodics, painkillers, and tranquilizers—all to no avail. Then a viral infection in the lining of my lungs created suffocating pain that took me to the emergency room of the nearest hospital.

There was no Mind/Body Clinic for me to go to back then, but there was a friend in the lab where I conducted my graduate research who was excited about his new hobby—meditation. He compared it to a mini-vacation in which he could switch off his cares and concerns and come out refreshed and ready to tackle whatever came up. My first thought was that meditation was for ascetics who lived in caves. I was a hard-headed scientist, literally killing myself to master the ways of the medical establishment.

Nevertheless, I gave it a try—largely out of desperation—practicing each day. The test came a few weeks later while I was sitting at an electron microscope, trying to unlock the secrets of cancer cells. I felt the familiar stabbing behind my right eye, the light sensitivity and nausea that heralded a migraine. It was time for an experiment.

Retreating to my office, I pulled the shades and shut the door. I settled into a chair, relaxed my muscles from head to foot, shifted my breathing from tense chest breathing to relaxed diaphragmatic breathing, and began to meditate. In time the pain subsided. After the meditation was over, I was left with a feeling of having been washed clean, like the earth after a heavy rain. I ran around the laboratory announcing that I had performed the most important experiment of my life. It was the beginning of a great change in my life.

In the following chapters, you'll share my journey of healing and some of those of the more than 2,000 patients* we've worked with at the Mind/Body Clinic, patients who have become in many ways my teachers.

---

*To honor their privacy, their names have been changed, as have any details that could identify them. At times the experiences of more than one patient have been combined in a single story.

Our patients range in age from seventeen to ninety-three, and they come from all walks of life. Their struggles and victories have been inspirations and challenges that constantly push me beyond the limits of what I know. Our patients are people who want to participate in their own healing but are wary of fads and unproven claims. They're students, executives, housewives, physicians, laborers, scientists, and engineers, and they come with migraine, insomnia, hives, ulcers, allergies, chronic pain, and more serious illnesses such as cancer and AIDS. They are referred by physicians, often after years of suffering and sometimes after endless rounds of medications that have not worked. As a rule, other therapies have failed because they address only the physical symptoms rather than the underlying causes.

Although the problems of a stressed overachiever may appear very different from those of a young mother suffering from multiple sclerosis and different still from those of an older man with cancer, all face similar crises. The underlying issues have as much to do with the meaning of life as with learning to use the power of the mind to reduce symptoms.

Recent major studies indicate that approximately seventy-five percent of visits to the doctor are either for illnesses that will ultimately get better by themselves or for disorders related to anxiety and stress. For these conditions, symptoms can be reduced or cured as the body's own natural healing balance is reinstated. For many other chronic or potentially life-threatening disorders, symptoms may be lessened, but the progress of disease will lead inevitably toward death. Death, after all, is part of the natural progression of life, and its reality can be a powerful reminder to live life in a way that maximizes contentment, creativity, and love. This is what I call healing. And the underlying desire for healing—for wholeness—is what every one of our patients has in common, regardless of the condition that brings them to the clinic.

In the chapters ahead you'll read about people who seem like yourself and others who seem very different. In the end, what is so miraculous to many of my patients is that, despite our differences, we're all alike. Beyond identities and desires there is a common core of self—an essential humanity whose nature is peace and whose expression is thought and whose action is unconditional love. When we identify with that inner core, respecting and honoring it in others as well as ourselves, we experience healing in every area of life.

The techniques we use with patients in our ten-week program are surprisingly simple, and in this book I will teach them to you in the same way we've taught them to thousands of others over the years. I hope that you will have the same positive outcome that they have had. Our research shows that people who have completed even a short six-week version of the program have a significant reduction in physical symptoms and a simultaneous decline in anxiety, depression, anger, fatigue, and irritability—a change that is lasting when they are retested six months later.

But The Mind/Body Program is not a quick fix, and it's not a miracle cure. Changing attitudes and ways of living is a demanding process, and while the techniques are simple, the issues are subtle and complex. Much of our success with patients rests on the credibility of the research on which our work is based. Because we work hand-in-hand with traditional medicine, our patients are confident that they are getting the best in medical care, rather than engaging in yet another unproved alternative. This a powerful motivation for them to make the changes that will lead to healing.

The message of this book, simply put, is that we are already perfect—our essential core is peaceful and whole. The work of healing is in peeling away the barriers of fear and past conditioning that keep us unaware of our true nature of wholeness and love. An artist who had carved an exquisitely intricate elephant was asked the secret of his talent. His answer was simple—he just chipped away the part of the stone that wasn't the elephant. The secret of minding the body and mending the mind is similar—chipping away at doubt and fear, we uncover our own birthright of inner peace. Discovering the peaceful inner core, in turn, brings the body back to wholeness or allows us to live well in spite of our physical limitations.

Presenting the material that leads to the discovery and understanding of this simple message in a book, rather than through personal interaction with groups of patients over a period of weeks, has been a fascinating challenge. Each reader is different, just as each patient is different. Honoring that individual is the key to learning. With that in mind, be flexible with yourself as you work along with the book. You may want to skim the book first for content and then go back and experience the techniques, mastering the tools at your own pace. Alternatively, you might wish to read through quite slowly, taking eight or ten weeks to work along with the program as if you were actually in a Mind/Body Group. You might even enjoy setting aside two hours once a week to work with the book, practicing the techniques you have learned during the week before moving on to the next chapter.

The chapters parallel the Mind/Body Program as it is delivered in the clinic. We begin with a lecture on mind/body interactions that is supplemented by workbook readings. I often suggest to patients that they read the scientific background material at their own pace, over several weeks if they prefer. Some patients are hungry for more and ask for guidance in reading the scientific literature. Some don't feel called upon to engage in the science at all. Others are somewhere in the middle. In writing the first chapter of this book, I decided to give as much scientific background as concisely as I could. Like the people who come to the clinic, you may find it is too much for you or just right or too little. In the first case, you may wish to skim this chapter lightly, coming back to it later if you feel the need. In the last case, you can supplement the material from the reading list provided at the end of the text.

Chapters 2 and 3 cover the content of the first four weeks of the clinic. I think of this material as a foundation—building the skill of becoming aware of how to mind the body. In these foundation chapters you will learn how to elicit the relaxation response through meditation, breathing, and stretching exercises. The practice of these exercises has two purposes. First, you learn to shift your physiology, gaining control of the stress response and learning to control the autonomic, or automatic, nervous system, as well as learning to let go of tension in the musculoskeletal system. Second, these basic skills begin to train you in the art of observing your mind.

Chapter 4 is a bridge between the fundamental skills of minding the body and the more advanced skills of mastering the mind. It concerns a critical area that all my patients immediately relate to—the ability to live life in the moment rather than being wrapped up in memories of the past or worries about the future. The ability to practice mindfulness rests on practicing the concentration and breathing exercises that come in the preceding chapters.

Chapters 5 and 6 provide tools for becoming an observer of the mind in a way that allows for a gradual process of waking up to the present by cutting through the conditioning of the past. This work culminates in learning to learn from emotions and to practice present-centered awareness—forgiveness—in daily life as introduced in Chapter 7.

The principles presented in the book are brought together in a very personal way in the last chapter, which tells Sam's story, a true life drama of mind and spirit overcoming the final limitation of the body—death itself. Sam's struggle with AIDS was a powerful healing experience in my own life and in the lives of many who knew him.

Before beginning the program, I suggest that you turn to the appendix and complete the self-evaluation of your current physical and emotional state. After finishing the book, when you feel that you understand the ideas and methods, you can re-evaluate your well-being by filling out the assessment a second time. The two questionnaires included are based on the actual evaluation that our patients complete in the clinic. Most people find the self-assessment helpful because it makes them more aware of their physical and emotional state. Completing them takes only a few minutes and will add to your self-understanding.

Each patient who enters a Mind/Body Group comes with a letter of referral from his or her physician so that we can make sure that the patient is getting the best of care and that no physical problem requiring medical intervention is overlooked. As part of the initial meeting, we often refer patients for additional help, be it medical or psychological. Therefore, in going through the self-evaluation materials, use them as an opportunity to ask yourself whether you need medical or psychological help in addition to self-help. A book like this is a wonderful adjunct in some cases, or it may be enough by itself, but it's always a good idea to ask for professional help if you have questions.

My own journey of healing began some twenty years ago and is still in progress. I hope that my experiences and those of the patients I have learned from and shared with will help you along your way. You may find the precepts of the book challenging, but they are a guidepost for a lifetime. I wish you well on your journey to healing and peace of mind.

1

The Science of Healing

Several years ago at the Tufts University School of Medicine, I saw an incredible movie demonstrating acupuncture anesthesia. As assistants twirled a few needles, a surgeon incised a patient's chest, cracked the ribs, and removed a lobe of the lung—all while the patient, his head demurely hidden behind a sheet, talked amiably and sipped tea. I was watching with my husband, immunologist Dr. Myrin Borysenko, and we were both astounded by what we saw. I could only shake my head when Myrin asked a colleague of ours from the medical school what he thought. "It's nothing," our colleague said. "Just hypnosis."

Until the last few years, scientists often have been in the position of having to deny what they were seeing, simply because the underlying mechanisms were not understood. Science is a search for explanations, a complex structure built of small, measurable units, yet some things that happen to real people in the real world just don't fit inside the well-established categories.

An individual with multiple personalities is diabetic in one identity but normal in all the others. A subject under hypnosis raises a very real blister on her skin, even though the "hot iron" the hypnotist says he is touching her with is, in reality, an ordinary pencil. In a clinical test, one-third of women receiving placebos instead of chemotherapy still lose their hair. How can this be?

The Power of Faith and Hope

Two thousand years ago a woman who had suffered prolonged uterine bleeding approached Jesus of Nazareth. Coming up to him in a crowd, she touched the hem of his garment and was instantly healed. Jesus turned to her and explained that it was her faith that had made her whole. After centuries of slow progress toward rational explanations of the physical world, even scientists can at last begin to appreciate the truth of His assessment. We are entering a new level in the scientific understanding of mechanisms by which faith, belief, and imagination can actually unlock the mysteries of healing.

In the late 1950s, Dr. Bruno Klopfer was treating a patient with an advanced, widespread lymphoma, a serious cancer of the immune system. The now discredited drug Krebiozen was being touted at the time as a potential cure, and shortly after Dr. Klopfer administered the drug, the patient's cancerous growths "melted like snowballs." The patient was released from the hospital, apparently free of disease. A few months later, when newspapers began to carry accounts of the worthlessness of the drug, the patient's tumors promptly recurred. Suspecting that the agent at work was the patient's belief, Klopfer announced that he would give him a specially prepared, more active form of the drug. In fact, he treated his patient with distilled water, yet once again the tumors melted away. In a few more months definitive studies were published showing beyond a doubt that Krebiozen was worthless. The patient became disillusioned, his tumors reappeared, and he quickly died.

Patients of the same age, sex, and physical status undergoing the same therapy often fare very differently with the same cancer. While an average time of survival can be determined, some people live much longer than expected and others die far more quickly than predicted. Numerous studies have shown that attitude may be a mechanism of profound importance in determining the course of at least some cancers.

In one study done by Dr. Steven Greer and his collaborators at the King's College Hospital in England, the attitude of fifty-seven women treated with mastectomy for early-stage breast cancer was related to survival ten years later. Of the women who faced the disease with a fighting spirit or whose denial was so strong that they believed there was no disease, fifty-five percent were alive and well after ten years. Among the women who felt hopeless and helpless or who stoically accepted their fate, only twenty-two percent were alive after ten years.

A study done by Dr. Yujiro Ikemi and his colleagues in Kyoto, Japan, centered on a small group of survivors from cancers usually considered incurable. The patients all told a similar story. Their reaction to the diagnosis was one of sincere gratitude for whatever life they might have remaining. They focused on the glass as half full rather than half empty. The cancer had appeared in all five patients at a time of severe existential crisis. The patients had reframed their crises as an opportunity to resolve the issues that led up to them. They were challenged by, and accepted responsibility for, their situations. Finally, all the patients completely and sincerely committed themselves to the will of God.

Sincere faith and belief are often associated with the few well-documented cases of seemingly spontaneous remissions. In 1976 Dr. B. J. Kennedy and his co-workers at the University of Minnesota Medical School studied twenty-two patients with supposedly incurable cancers who had recovered and lived for at least five years. They had similar attitudes. After they recovered from their initial shock, they were determined to fight and win. They firmly believed in recovery. Many cited the importance of knowing that even one other person had survived with their type of cancer. If someone else could survive, why couldn't they? Patients cited their belief in their doctors, in medical science, and in God. The key factor was that they had strong faith in something that prevented them from feeling helpless. There are countless such examples of the mind's power over the body. We are only beginning to understand the science behind them and the importance of feeling hopeful and in control.

Mind and Immunity

My roots and those of the Mind/Body Clinic are in laboratory research. The effect of mind on immunity is a research interest that I share with my husband, Myrin. The immune system, the body's front line of defense against disease; the cardiovascular system; the brain and nervous system—all have been explored independently. In recent years, however, neuroscientists working with psychologists and immunologists have forged a new scientific discipline with the tongue-twisting name of psychoneuroimmunology, or PNI, a field that explores the body's most subtle interconnections.

Much PNI research centers on a group of hormonal messengers called *neuropeptides,* which are secreted by the brain, by the immune system, and by the nerve cells in various other organs. What scientists have found is that the areas of the brain that control emotion are particularly rich in receptors for these chemicals. At the same time, the brain also has receptor sites for molecules produced by the immune system alone—the lymphokines and interleukins. What we see, then, is a rich and intricate two-way communication system linking the mind, the immune system, and potentially all other systems, a pathway through which our emotions—our hopes and fears—can affect the body's ability to defend itself.

In the 1940s, Swiss physiologist and Nobel laureate Walter Hesse experimented on the cat brain and discovered that he could produce two diametrically opposed energy states simply by stimulating different areas of the animal's hypothalamus. One state was a kind of "passing gear" for heightened activity; the other was a state of very low energy expenditure characterized by deep rest and relaxation—the bodily equivalent of "neutral."

More recently, Dr. R. Keith Wallace and my colleague Dr. Herbert Benson documented a similar state of profound rest in humans who practiced transcendental meditation. Benson's subsequent studies proved that this state could be elicited through any form of mental concentration that distracted the individual from the usual cares and concerns of the mind. He termed this innate, hypothalamic mechanism the *relaxation response*.

When the relaxation response is called on, heart rate and blood pressure drop. Breathing rate and oxygen consumption decline because of the profound decrease in the need for energy. Brain waves shift from an alert beta-rhythm to a relaxed alpha-rhythm. Blood flow to the muscles decreases, and instead, blood is sent to the brain and skin, producing a feeling of warmth and rested mental alertness. It was by learning to induce the relaxation response that I began to reverse symptoms that were severe enough to send me to the emergency room.

How was it that stress was able to bring on these symptoms in the first place? Scientists know that the relaxation response evolved as a means of protecting the organism from burnout. Nature also provided the "passing gear" we call the fight-or-flight response. I'm sure you've felt it many times when you were suddenly afraid, when you were sure someone was breaking into the house, or when the plane you were on suddenly dropped as it hit a pocket of air. Before you knew it, you were breathing fast and shallow, your palms were sweaty, and your mouth was dry. The fight-or-flight response means your heart is pounding, your blood pressure is up, your muscles are tense, your pupils are dilated, and your skin is covered with goose bumps.

This integrated response evolved millions of years ago because it ensured that the whole organism would be ready for action at the slightest hint of danger. The response is still with us today, hard wired into the human body's communication systems, even though in our infinitely more complex world, danger can take the form of unpaid bills or boredom in a marriage or some unspoken dread produced entirely by the imagination. Fighting and fleeing are not very useful options against such dangers. Nevertheless, through the fight-or-flight response, anxiety still has access to the pathway that elevates blood pressure, and stress still activates pathways that lead to muscle tension and thereby to numerous aches, pains, and bodily disorders.

Anxiety has still other ways of making us more prone to illness. In laboratory experiments, we've learned that stress, whether acute or chronic, releases a whole array of hormones that provide quick energy. Two of these hormones—adrenalin and cortisol—are also potent inhibitors of the immune system.

In an experiment he was doing at the Tufts Medical School, my husband, Myrin, needed a particular kind of antibody—those proteins the body produces to help neutralize foreign invaders such as microbes. Scientists usually obtain antibodies by injecting rabbits with the specific foreign protein—the antigen—for which they're hoping to get the antibody. For months Myrin checked the rabbits' blood samples, but the antibody he was looking for never appeared. Frustrated but determined to consider all possibilities, he went to the animal facility and found that, while the rabbits seemed comfortable enough, there was a massive temperature recorder next to the cages. After each minute the recorder would click. After each click the rabbits would thump—a danger signal. Myrin's assumption was that the rabbits were chronically stressed and therefore their immune reactions were suppressed.

Following the same line of thought, Dr. Bruce Crary, Dr. Herbert Benson, Myrin, and I conducted a study in which we injected human volunteers with a tiny dose of adrenalin—about the amount you'd produce if someone yelled "Boo!" What we found was an immediate decline in the helper cells, lymphocytes that augment the immune response.

Why should stress sometimes decrease immunity? Some scientists find an explanation by once again looking back in evolutionary history to the most stressful event in an animal's life—the danger of a bloody attack by a predator. They reason that damaged tissue from a wound could be mistaken by the immune system as foreign cells, resulting in an immunological catastrophe—an immune reaction launched against the self. In anticipation of trauma, then, the stressed immune system takes a temporary dip.

A fascinating psychological twist to this phenomenon came to light in a study of dental students that Myrin and I did in collaboration with Dr. John Jemmott, Dr. David McClelland, Dr. Herbert Benson, and others. We discovered that the stress of examination periods reduced the level of a particular antibody in saliva, an antibody that is part of the first line of defense against colds. Exam time is typically when students are most likely to catch colds, but the more important finding for our work was that the students who in psychological testing showed the greatest need for power were the ones with the greatest drop in antibodies! The exams were much more a threat to them than to students with a more easygoing approach to life.

Other studies at Ohio State Medical School done by Dr. Janice Kiecolt-Glaser and her husband, Dr. Ronald Glaser, showed that exam stress decreased the function of an important type of lymphocyte called the natural killer cell. These cells are responsible for patrolling the body and destroying virus-infected cells as well as cancer cells. Exam stress also caused a precipitous decline in the production of interferon, a molecule that boosts the function of natural killer cells and other types of immune cells.

Disease, however, is rarely a simple matter of isolated cause and effect. While stress and helplessness can depress immune function, clearly we don't get sick each time we're stressed. It's far more reasonable to consider stress as one of many factors that may tip the balance toward illness.

Each of the mechanisms I've discussed—the hormonal messengers linking the brain and the immune system, the fight-or-flight response, immunosuppression, and the relaxation response—function in bodies subject to three other important determinants of well-being: heredity, environment, and behavior.

Some people are constitutionally lucky; their genes are programmed for health and longevity. Others, less fortunate, are genetically predisposed to high blood pressure, diabetes, or multiple sclerosis. Even so, many people with a possible genetically linked disease stay well. In my own case, one behavior—the relaxation response—buffered the genetic pattern of hyperarousal in my family that contributes to high blood pressure and migraines. For others, changing something in the environment such as diet can prevent the expression of migraines or hypertension or alter the level of immune response.

The one factor that has links to every determinant of health, other than hard-wired genetic constitution, is, of course, behaviors. We decide about our health habits— whether we exercise, what we eat, whether we smoke or drink. Just as important, our minds have the ability to spin out endless imaginings that are quite real to the body, imaginings that unleash the hormones and neuropeptides that tell the body what to do. Most of us are unable to control even those negative mental fantasies of which we are conscious. Worse still, we're often unaware of what is going through our mind. In the chapters that follow, you will learn how the mind works and how to control it in a way that maximizes your health.

Mind/Body Programming

Every time you miss your exit on the highway because you are daydreaming, then "wake up" to discover yourself miles farther down the road, you are demonstrating the power of the unconscious mind. Once something is learned, we don't have to think about it consciously. The task simply repeats itself as soon as we initiate the program—in this case, by putting the key in the ignition. The rest of driving is second nature because our nervous system has been conditioned—or imprinted—with the driving pattern.

Because of our conditioning, we are all creatures of habit. Most people get anxious before taking an exam partly because they have become habituated to feeling anxious at exam time, whether or not the situation at hand is actually threatening. Once threatened by an exam, a neural connection is established. The next time an exam comes up, the probability is that we'll reactivate that same conditioned circuit.

Physiological conditioning is a kind of rapid learning that evolved to help us master cause-and-effect situations that might determine survival. We all are familiar with Pavlov's famous experiment. A dog is given meat powder, which naturally makes him salivate. A bell is then rung every time the meat powder is presented. After a time the dog salivates merely at the sound of the bell. We see the same mechanism operating in ourselves when we're working away contentedly, then glance up at the clock, notice it's lunch time, and suddenly become hungry.

The mind's power to affect the body through conditioning became crystal clear to me when I was six or seven years old. My Uncle Dick, a confirmed cheese hater, was eating Sunday dinner with us. For dessert there was a cheesecake camouflaged with ripe strawberries. It was so good that he ate two pieces. About an hour later my mother expressed her surprise at Uncle Dick's delight in the dessert, since she knew how much he hated cheese. At the sound of the word *cheese*, Uncle Dick turned pale, began to gag, and ran for the bathroom. Even as a child it was obvious to me that the problem was not the cheese itself, but some mental conditioning about cheese that produced such a violent reaction.

Many people who receive chemotherapy for cancer get sick to their stomachs from the medication. Soon, through conditioning similar to Uncle Dick's, they begin to get sick before they actually receive the drugs. Some people begin to get nauseous the night before treatment. Others may get nauseous coming to the hospital or even upon seeing their doctor or nurse. They have involuntarily learned to get sick as a conditioned response to the thoughts, sights, and smells of the chemotherapy situation.

What we've learned from Soviet studies following Pavlov's model is that the immune system itself can be conditioned. In this country Dr. Robert Ader and Dr. Nicholas Cohen at the University of Rochester injected rats with an immunosuppressant drug called cyclophosphamide and at the same time added a new taste—saccharin—to the animals' drinking water. The saccharin acted like Pavlov's bell. After a while the rats were suppressing their immunity at the taste of saccharin alone.

Dr. G. Richard Smith and Sandra McDaniel did a fascinating study of the suppression of immune reactions in humans. Once a month for five months, volunteers who had reacted positively in a tuberculin skin test came into the same room with the same arrangement of furniture and the same nurse. Each time they saw a red and green vial on the desk, and each time the contents of the red vial—tuberculin—were injected into the same arm, and the contents of the green vial—a salt solution—were injected into the other.

Month after month the same procedure was followed, and month after month the volunteers had the same reaction to the tuberculin—a red swollen patch on the same arm. There was never any reaction to the injection of the salt solution in the other arm.

On the sixth trial the contents of the vials were switched without the volunteers' knowledge. And this time the volunteers had almost no reaction to the tuberculin. Their expectation that nothing ever happened after the injection from the green vial apparently was enough to inhibit the immune system's powerful inflammatory response to tuberculin.

Conditioning is a powerful bridge between mind and body, and a primary focus of our work at the clinic. The reason is that the body cannot tell the difference between events that are actual threats to survival and events that are present in thought alone. The mind spins out endless fantasies of possible disasters past and future. This tendency to escalate a situation into its worst possible conclusion is what I call awfulizing, and it can be a key factor in tipping the balance toward illness or health. Perhaps you're hung up in traffic, sure to be late for an important 9 A.M. meeting. Or it's midnight and your child is still out, or the doctor tells you she wants to repeat a test, or so on in endless variation. The flood of "what ifs" and "if onlys" engages the various human emotions, which can influence virtually all bodily functions.

The way our minds work—the degree to which we awfulize—also depends on previous conditioning. The responses of our parents and other influential role models shape our own reactions to life. Awareness of our conditioning is the first step toward unlearning attitudes that have outlived their usefulness. Such awareness opens our ability to respond to what is happening *now* rather than reacting out of a conditioned history that may be archaic. This is the skill you will learn if you really apply yourself to the techniques outlined in the following chapters.

The Dangers of Helplessness

The acute stresses of life produce temporary physiological responses from which the body recovers. It's the chronic stresses—often caused by conditioned negative attitudes and feelings of helplessness—that are the real challenge to healing. Feeling constantly helpless can upset our endocrine balance, elevating the immunosuppressant hormone cortisol and destroying its natural diurnal rhythm. Chronic helplessness also depletes the brain of the vital neurotransmitter norepinephrine, the chemical in our brains that is necessary for feelings of happiness and contentment. Immunological studies, too, reveal that the inability to feel in control of stress, rather than the stressful event itself, is the most damaging to immunity.

Most of us eventually will feel that life is out of control in some way. Whether we see this as a temporary situation whose resolution will add to our store of knowledge and experience or as one more threat demonstrating life's dangers is the most crucial question both for the quality of our life and our physical health.

Our ability to create the conditions of life most dear to us—realizing our hopes and dreams, goals and aspirations—depends on having control both over events that we initiate ourselves and over those that come into our lives unbidden—the seeming stresses, obstacles, and disappointments. Without the conviction that we have some control, we have no way to negotiate the tides of life.

In the early 1970s, psychologist Jay Weiss exposed two rats to the same stress—a mild shock to the tail—in a situation where only one of the rats had control of the stress. A third rat served as a comparison and was not shocked at all. The first rat learned that by rotating a wheel he could turn off the shock, both for himself and for the second rat. In this way both rats got exactly the same amount of stress, but the difference was that one rat could control the situation while the other was helpless. The helpless rats developed ulcers twice as large as those of the rats who had control.

Unpredictability is closely related to uncontrollability. If rats were signaled with a beeping noise for ten seconds before the shock came on, they had much less severe ulcers. Knowing when to anticipate the stress allowed the rats to relax during the "safe" periods, reducing the wear and tear of chronic anxiety, which is really chronic fight-or-flight.

People who feel in control of life can withstand an enormous amount of change and thrive on it. People who feel helpless can hardly cope at all. Almost everyone knows people of both sorts. The truly imperturbable types might be represented by James Bond, because 007 is nothing if not stress hardy. Bombs explode around him as he parachutes into the supervillain's diabolical nuclear reactor, but he calmly combs his hair and picks lint off his navy blazer. On the other hand, there are the emotionally fragile male protagonists in Woody Allen films. Insecure and awfulizing relentlessly about how bad things could get, Allen's characters are prone to develop ulcers when faced with what to order for dessert. The potential hazards of helplessness and emotional repression didn't escape Marshall Brinkman and Woody Allen in their script of *Manhattan*. In it, Allen plays one of his typical retiring males. Diane Keaton, playing his girlfriend, announces that she is leaving Allen for his best friend. When the Allen character looks unperturbed, Keaton becomes agitated, demanding to know why he doesn't react. He sighs and tells her that he can't express anger. "I grow a tumor instead," he says.

Psychologist Martin Seligman from the University of Pennsylvania points out that our ability to develop control begins in infancy, when the good mother mirrors and responds to the actions of her child. Baby smiles, mother smiles. Baby coos, mother coos. Baby cries with hunger, and mother responds with milk. Through this "dance of development," the infant learns that it has control, that it can ensure its own survival.

Human infants raised in some institutionalized environments are deprived of this dance of development. They have no control since they are fed on schedule, changed on schedule, and have little interaction with caretakers. Previously happy infants become weepy. After a few months they stop crying and become withdrawn, staring at the wall. At first they ignore people who approach them; later they begin to shriek. They lose weight, often develop insomnia, and are very prone to infections. Many die before they are three years old.

If no control is possible, then helplessness sets in. If your actions and responses don't make any difference, if you have no impact on the world, why bother? The person who has experienced helplessness in one situation is more likely to act helplessly in other situations. He or she has been conditioned.

Seligman contends that we learn to be helpless, and the resultant depressed behavior then feeds on itself. Helplessness is characterized by a decreased motivation to do anything about life's difficulties and by a negative mind-set that makes it hard to appreciate that you did something right when you actually do change a situation. Emotionally there is anxiety as long as you are trying to control an unpredictable situation, then depression and giving up when the situation seems beyond control.

Hardiness: Overcoming Helplessness

Life is filled with changes. It's whether we can cope with those changes or not that determines whether we will grow with the situation or be overcome by it, whether we will act helplessly or have hope. Dr. Suzanne Kobasa and her colleagues have studied the difference between these two extremes. In studies of business executives and lawyers, Kobasa first found that those with a great deal of life stress could be protected from physical illness by a combination of three attitudes which together describe the stress-hardy personality. *Commitment* is an attitude of curiosity and involvement in whatever is happening. Its opposite is alienation—as seen in the children in foundling homes who have withdrawn from the world. The second attitude is *control,* which we have seen is the opposite of helplessness. It is the belief that we can influence events, coupled with the willingness to act on that belief rather than be a victim of circumstances. The third is *challenge,* the belief that life's changes stimulate personal growth instead of threatening the status quo.

The attitudes of hardiness lead to a kind of coping that Kobasa calls transformational. Committed people who believe they are in control and expect situations to be challenging are likely to react to stressful events by *increasing* their interaction with them—exploring, controlling, and learning from them. This attitude transforms the event into something less stressful by placing it in a broader frame of reference that revolves around continued personal growth and understanding.

Persons low in hardiness, those conditioned to be helpless, are likely to engage in what Kobasa calls regressive coping. Like the foundling home infants, regressive copers back away from stress and dwell instead on their own repetitive emotional reactions. Their attitudes are the opposite of hardiness. They are alienated from activities, feel powerless to change things, and are therefore threatened by anything that rocks the boat. These people are the ones who are the most likely to fall ill when stressful events arise.

Harvard psychiatrist Dr. George Vaillant, in a landmark study reported in his book *Adaptation to Life*, showed that mental health is the most important predictor of physical health. He analyzed data collected about the lives and mental and physical health of a group of Harvard alumni over a period of thirty years. He found that men with immature coping styles, similar to regressive coping, became ill four times more often than men with hardier styles.

We are now beginning to understand some of the mechanisms underlying the erosion of health by poor coping. We are unraveling the intricate effect of chronic stress on hormones, neuropeptides, and the central nervous system, which in turn can affect every system of the body, from the immune to the cardiovascular. The effects of stress are buffered by effective coping and also by the love and support of other people. Vaillant found that lonely men often became chronically ill by the time they reached their fifties. It's only through our relations with others that we develop the outlook of hardiness and come to believe in our own capabilities and inner goodness. The lonely baby is in no position to become hardy. The lonely adult may have problems sustaining the attitudes of hardiness.

Several years ago, the small town of Roseto, Pennsylvania, raised considerable interest in the scientific community because of its very low rate of death from coronary heart disease. Epidemiologists began to study the Rosetans, expecting to find low levels of the major risk factors for coronary heart disease: cigarette smoking, fat consumption, a sedentary lifestyle, and obesity. They got a big surprise. The Rosetans had terrible health habits. They were high in all the risk factors. It turned out that their protective factor was actually the social fabric of the community. The extended family was alive and well. People tended to stay within Roseto, and so there was a great deal of closeness. People knew one another, their family histories, their joys and sorrows. In Roseto there were plenty of people to listen and to lend a hand when needed. Statistics revealed that when people moved out of Roseto, their rate of heart attack rose to the predicted level. Social support, the great stress buffer, turned out to be more important than health habits in predicting heart disease.

We've always known that we can literally die of broken hearts and shattered dreams. Laboratory findings are now corroborating that intuitive sense. The most pressing question for us, then, is how to reconnect with hope, faith, and love, and how to use these states for minding the body and mending the mind.

How can we overcome conditioning that often causes us to close down in fear rather than open up in love? At the heart of the process are the techniques we'll turn to in the next three chapters—meditation, breath control, and mindfulness—through which we can reach an internal balance point where the mind becomes still. In the state of stillness, the physiology shifts into the relaxation response. Negative conditioning circuits are derailed, and the mind is open to the formation of more productive habits.

In the coming chapters you will learn to reach that balance point, becoming aware of your own limiting mind habits and their effect on your body. You will be able to prevent the automatic, conditioned responses that lead to stress and physical illness by creating new circuits that activate your own inner healing potential. You will learn the attitudes of stress hardiness—reframing life's stresses as challenges, which is the key to breaking away from helplessness and regaining control of body and mind.

A side effect of this program of healing is a reconnection to the values that are most important in life: an openness to love, an attitude of forgiveness toward ourselves and others, and peace of mind. Without peace of mind, life is just a shadow of its possibilities. The most beautiful scene leaves you empty if your mind is full of worry. Even the arms of your beloved seem remote. One of my meditation teachers put it very clearly when he said that all the experiences of life are like zeros in a long number. They are meaningless without a digit in front of them. That digit is peace of mind.

2

Getting Back in Control

The paradox of control is simple. The more we try to control life, the less control we have. Several summers ago I watched an adorable little boy, probably about four years old, playing at the beach. He had built a sand castle with a moat around it when the tide was out. As the tide moved in, a wave would occasionally break close enough for some water to trickle into the moat and fill it. The child was delighted his invention worked. But as the tide continued to rise, the waves lapped at the castle, threatening destruction. The child began frantically to pile up sand in front of the castle, building a dike to deflect the flood. He was caught in a constant struggle of breaking down and building up.

Several yards down the beach, a girl of about the same age began a parallel struggle, but not for long. She soon recognized the inevitability of the tide and moved on to a game of digging holes at the tide line, watching them fill with water and erode and then moving back. The first child ended up angry and frustrated—his castle had been destroyed in spite of every effort to control the tides. The second child had instead discovered a new game and spent a doubly pleasant afternoon. She had both literally and figuratively learned to let go—to go with the flow.

Not knowing when to let go, throwing useless effort into protecting sand castles, is a major cause of stress and loss of creativity. As we saw in Chapter 1, feeling that we're in control is primary to health. On the other hand, if we try to control too tightly, we're likely to wind up like the little boy on the beach. How to resolve this paradox? Developing the discrimination to tell when to hold on and when to let go is the key to escaping past conditioning and responding freshly to life's challenges. This means being flexible and self-aware. The Japanese say that in a storm, it is the bamboo, the flexible tree, that can bend with the wind and survive. The rigid tree that resists the wind falls, victim of its own insistence to control.

Stress As Opportunity

It is hard to know how well we will manage until we are issued an invitation to stress. Shakespeare said, "When the sea was calm all boats alike showed mastership in floating." Only in a storm are they obliged to cope. Storms and struggles, chaos and tragedy have always been looked upon as the teachers of valuable, if unwelcome, lessons. In the struggle to survive a stressful situation, a new way of being often emerges that is much more satisfying than the old. Every religion and the great myths and fables of all cultures discuss change and growth through the archetypes of death and rebirth. Easter and Passover, symbolic of death and resurrection, are also metaphors for escape from our past conditioning and outmoded concepts—and rebirth into freedom. The phoenix that arises from its ashes and the seed that dies to give birth to the flower are all variations on the theme of life as a continuous process of growth. An endless round of little deaths and rebirths. Paul put it elegantly in the New Testament when he said, "I die daily."

Why, then do we hold on to the old so earnestly? What is the block to letting go in the moment? That block is fear—lack of faith in ourselves and in life. If I give up a bad relationship, maybe no one better will come along. If I look for a new job, maybe I will get a worse one. If I let go of my suspicion, maybe I will be hurt and disappointed by people. It is fear that masquerades as the need to control, and fear that deprives us of the chance to be free.

Most Americans don't like to think about pain and suffering. We are an optimistic people, inclined to think of the future as unfolding with endless promise. Usually we avoid pain until it hurts enough so that it can no longer be ignored. Buddhist philosophy revolves around the inevitability of suffering in human life. The first of the Four Noble Truths states quite simply that life is suffering. The other truths discuss how attitudes create suffering and how those attitudes can be changed.

The process of facing change in a stress-hardy manner by allowing it to be an opportunity rather than a threat can be accomplished by anyone who wants to learn. Here is how to begin.

Step 1: Willing to Be Aware

My mother once assured me that ignorance is bliss. What you don't think about can't hurt you. This coping style is popular indeed, but it's a great description of regressive coping, which ensures stress and prevents change.

People do the best they can to get through life comfortably. No normal person knowingly creates suffering. The walls of protection that we build against awareness of our suffering seem like a good idea. The trouble is that they keep us prisoners of our own misconceptions. Children are often frightened in the dark because they mistake harmless things, like the shadow of a shirt hanging over the back of a chair, for horrible monsters. Some have the courage to turn on the light and have a look. They are the lucky ones. Others can at least cry out for help, and they, too, become free of their illusions. But those who choose to hide under the covers, afraid even to breathe, are in the worst position of all. They are prisoners of their own imaginations.

When we grow older, it's not so easy to hide under the covers. Instead, we learn to hide from ourselves, from our own frightening thoughts and feelings. This is most easily accomplished by distraction—learning to ignore bad feelings by thinking of other things. Some people get so good that they can't remember the frightening feelings at all. Such denial is the cradle in which fear grows up. Fear makes your body tense. The mind responds by producing conditioned mental associations to tension. Thus, the types of distracting thoughts that form most likely will be worries and fears over other things.

One of my patients, a woman named Nancy, had a terrible marriage, but she couldn't admit it to herself. Her husband was an alcoholic. He was often withdrawn and sullen, rarely reaching out lovingly to her and their children. Nancy had long ago stopped talking to him about his drinking, since he'd call her a nag and denounce her as the one with the problem.

Nonetheless, they still cared for each other. She felt powerless and scared, but she rationalized her situation, hiding her true feelings. When we talked about her husband, at first she said he didn't drink *that* much. He was a pretty good father, a respectable professional, and really a sweet person at heart. They had been married for twenty years, much longer than many of their friends. She had pushed her fear and anger down very deep, which takes a lot of energy. This is the denial, the psychic equivalent of pulling the covers over your head. The price she paid was a state of chronic tension that showed up in two ways—physically as headaches, nausea, and insomnia and psychologically as compulsive behavior.

Nancy, who looked tired and aged beyond her forty-five years, was constantly concerned about her teenage children. They were great kids, but an unending parade of "What ifs" ran through her mind like squirrels. What if they got into a car accident, what if they got into drugs, what if they got mugged, raped, disappointed, sick, and so forth without stop. She couldn't turn off the worries when she lay down to sleep, so sleep became a serious problem. She tried to control all their comings and goings. It was only her physical ills that finally made her reach out for help and open up to an understanding of how her regressive coping was costing her both her health and peace of mind. Then she could learn what it means to really have control—to take responsibility for her marriage.

Worry shows up both mentally and physically—a perfect setup for the creation of a vicious cycle. Worried thoughts, whether conscious or repressed like Nancy's, create tension through the physiology of the fight-or-flight response. Physical tension narrows our mental focus and we tend to worry more. The cycle becomes self-sustaining. It is possible to worry about anything at all. Advanced worriers spend little time worrying about current problems. Instead, they choose from the endless buffet of past memories and future fantasies. Some become superstitious, with worrying becoming a talisman that prevents bad things from happening. It is awfully tiring to be scouting endlessly for danger, since our minds can create new dangers out of thin air. Awareness of our fears is the first step toward breaking out of the pattern of worry and overcontrol. Step Two is changing the mind-set that is conditioned to fear.

Step 2: Freeing the Inner Physician

Life naturally tends toward wholeness and growth. Even the inhospitable cracks in city sidewalks sustain seeds that will do their best to sprout, no matter what the condition. When our energy is tied up in useless worry and fight-or-flight, though, we oppose the natural tendency toward growth and wholeness. This is where the relaxation response comes in.

Its physiology is in itself healing, creating a state of lowered arousal of the sympathetic nervous system that diminishes many symptoms caused by or worsened by stress. Its action is twofold. Like a prescription drug, the relaxation response has a direct effect on the body and it has certain side effects. These side effects result from an awareness that helps us break through our conditioning.

Meditation is the way we learn to access the relaxation response and to be aware of the mind and the way in which our attitudes produce stress. This capacity to observe our own minds leads to stress hardiness. By provoking questioning about life's meanings, it develops a curiosity about things—a *commitment*. By teaching the mind to become aware and then to let go, meditation trains us in responsibility and appropriate *control*. By allowing the emergence of new attitudes, we develop the understanding that life's threats are better dealt with as *challenges*.

In addition to building stress hardiness, meditation also releases the inner physician by quieting the mind so that the body's own inner wisdom can be heard. My husband tells a story of immigrating to this country when he was about seven years old. Shortly after arriving, a girl of five made a beeline for an orange stand. She ate three or four oranges in a few minutes—a prodigious snack for such a small child. The little girl had endured physical and emotional conditions on her long trip that created a need for vitamin C. Scientists have long known that children whose appetites have not been dulled by sugar and rich, fatty foods will choose a perfectly balanced diet. This is the wisdom of the body.

At other times the body may need exercise, rest, or physical touch. When the body's inner wisdom is obscured by inattention through worry, the result is similar to having the appetite dulled by sweets—we cannot hear the prescription of the inner healer. Meditation, through its ability to help us navigate the mind, restores that ability of inner listening, allowing us to make the best choices.

When most of us tune in to the mind, listening to what passes through, we become aware of an insistent internal conversation with ourselves. That inner dialogue is the endless stream of thinking that comments on our experiences. We are often more tuned in to its commentary than we are to what's actually happening, with the result that we miss the moment. We live in endless variations of old reruns of the mind. If we were once frightened in a dark alley, we may always feel fright in dark alleys, even if there is no cause. As soon as the mind sees the alley, it reruns old tapes of fear and doubt. Regardless of reality, fear and doubt are what we feel. Because the storehouse of our past experience is so large, the inner dialogue has endless material out of which to shape a logical, safe description of the world.

Do you ever have trouble remembering someone's name right after you are introduced? Most people do. Instead of paying attention to the person's name, you think about things like what you will say, whether you are standing close enough to offend him with the garlic from last night's antipasto, whether she will like you, whether you will like her, how big his nose is, what color her clothes are, and so forth in endless variation. This thinking goes on without our awareness; you are "lost in thought" and are not "present" with what is actually going on, so you miss the name.

We all experience many such moments. We fly by the highway exit before we can notice it, or we stand in front of the refrigerator and can't remember why. We are literally out to lunch—and sadly it is often in a proverbial garbage heap of worries, fears, blame, and doubts.

The first step toward becoming conscious is learning to become aware of the constantly changing landscape of thoughts, feelings, and perceptions that constipate the mind and mask awareness of the inner physician. Lost in the inner dialogue, we are only partly awake, sleepwalking our way through life.

To develop a state of inner awareness, to witness and let go of the old dialogues, you need an observation point. If you went out in a boat to view offshore tides but neglected to put down an anchor, you would soon be carried off to sea. So it is with the mind. Without an anchor to keep the mind in place, it will be carried away by the torrent of thoughts. Your ability to watch what is happening will be lost. The practice of meditation, which calms the body through the relaxation response and fixes the mind through dropping the anchor of attention, is the most important tool of self-healing and self-regulation.

What Is Meditation?

Meditation is any activity that keeps the attention pleasantly anchored in the present moment. Think of an activity that you really enjoy. As I'm sitting here at the typewriter it is a hot summer day. I am sweating profusely and I fantasize for a moment. I approach a beautiful lake. I notice the trees, flowers, and grass. The wind is warm as it blows over me. Now I wade into the lake and then dive in. I pause and enjoy my own sense of the cooling water. Ahh. For a moment the world stops. I am no longer concerned with books, bills, shopping, relationships, or any other thoughts. I surrender to the immediate pleasure of the water. That's what enjoyment is. Surrender. Letting go of all the things pulling you out of the moment.

One of my patients named Sally had lost interest in her sex life. I asked her what she experienced in her mind during lovemaking. Sally told me that she and her husband made love on Saturday mornings. In her mind she usually got wrapped up in making a list of the day's events. She worked all week and Sunday was the time for church and family visits, so Saturday was the day for shopping, cleaning, and other errands. Since her mind was at the dry cleaner's, there was no one home to enjoy the sex!

To get back to a good sex life, Sally had to become aware of the causes of her problem—the time she and her husband had chosen and the way her mind reacted. She addressed both by taking action to change the time and by retraining her mind through meditation, in learning to surrender, to let go to the experience. *These two paths—taking action where required and surrendering when no further action is possible—are the paths to stress hardiness.*

Since all of us have periods of concentration, the state of meditation is actually quite familiar. It occurs whenever we are fully engaged in what we are doing. In all those cases, a shift occurs between what's in the foreground and what's in the background of the mind. Think about how you feel when you are really in the present moment with something. It may be skiing, swimming, reading a good book, making love, planting flowers—anything that holds your attention. Take a minute and remember this feeling. Peaceful, right?

For once, the mind is not reading its list of things that must happen before we can be happy. It's not reciting the list of awful things that could happen to steal our happiness. It has taken a back seat to *just being*. This is the meditative state that elicits the relaxation response. It is peace. As we'll discuss further in Chapter 4, the peaceful state that we're all looking for is present all the time. The problem is that we cannot appreciate it as long as the mind is in turmoil.

Learning to meditate is like learning to do anything. The first requirement is motivation. Without it, there is no energy to make the effort. For most of us, this is no problem. Stress, pain, suffering, no peace of mind—these adverse circumstances become opportunities because they force us to change.

The second requirement is effort. You must practice in order to learn. All the reading in the world isn't worth a week's practice. At a minimum, ten to twenty minutes a day are required to start getting the hang of meditation.

The third requirement is determination. Usually people quit anything when they decide that they'll never be any good at it. Meditation is no exception. Because you are zeroing in on your mind, what you'll notice at first is its turbulence, as well as its moments of peace. If you interpret the turbulence as "I can't do this," your mind has won using one of its favorite tricks, which you'll read about in Chapter 6.

I remember learning to jog. I was very out of shape. Ten years of heavy smoking had taken a toll on my lungs. Furthermore, I came from a family in which no one had ever heard of exercise; our idea of cardiovascular fitness was to increase the heart rate by drinking coffee and smoking cigarettes! At first, jogging was torture. Every step was proof I wasn't cut out for exercise. I was sustained, however, by the memory of a PBS program that featured an older woman who learned to jog and now ran forty miles a week. She had started by running to her mailbox and back—a few yards. Next, she jogged on the street, then walked until she recovered her breath. In a couple of months she could jog a mile, then two miles, until she got all the way up to eight miles at a time.

I was impressed. I was younger and a lot thinner. I had no excuses. As I jogged, my lungs would burn and my legs ache. My mind would say, "I told you, Joan, all Zakons [my maiden name] have small lungs; you will never do this." I had a secret weapon, however, because I knew how to meditate and win the battle of the mind by ignoring it. On every in breath I repeated the phrase "If she can do it," and on every out breath I repeated "so can I." And I could. After a few months, even out-of-shape me could run for five miles.

Remember, *when practicing, just do it: don't get discouraged.* It took years for your mind to build its scaffolding of tricks and worries. It will take time to dismantle them. *Don't evaluate your performance.* Like the beginning jogger, you should think, "Great—I did it." Not "It was a great jog" or a rotten jog. It was a jog. That's enough.

You already know that meditation is nothing more than anchoring your attention in the present. That's exactly what I was doing in the jogging example. Instead of becoming lost in my mind's complaints, I focused on breathing. Breathing is a neutral focus that is with us every moment of the day. Breathing is an anchor, or focus, common to many traditional forms of meditation. To anchor the mind even more firmly, a word or phrase is often added, repeated silently in time to the breathing. "If she can do it . . . so can I" is a good example of the focus phrases, often called mantras, used in meditation. They are like brooms, sweeping the mind clear of other thoughts.

Focus words can be neutral, meaningless sounds or meaningful phrases. In Dr. Herbert Benson's recent book, *Beyond the Relaxation Response: The Faith Factor*, he writes about the power of a person's belief and how it can support the practice of meditation. When Dr. Benson surveyed world literature, both secular and nonsecular, for instructions on meditation, he found a traditional Japanese approach that used counting as a focus. You breathe in and out on the count of one. On the next breath you move to two and so forth until you get to ten. Then you count back down to one over the next ten breaths.

When Dr. Benson tried this in a laboratory experiment with student volunteers, he got an unexpected result. The students became so flustered when they repeatedly lost count that they could not elicit the relaxation response. All he was able to measure was their performance anxiety. He told them to forget counting and just stick with the word *one*. Breathe in, breathe out, and repeat *one* on each out breath. That worked fine, and he was able to document the physiological effects of meditation.

The same word, though, will not be appropriate for everyone. Take my first patient. Alan, a computer company executive, came to the clinic to learn the relaxation response to counteract the nausea and vomiting of the chemotherapy he was receiving for cancer. We shut our eyes and I had him relax his body. I instructed him to just follow his breathing, repeating the word *one* on each out breath. After a few minutes of this, I could hear that he was breathing faster than before, and when I opened my eyes, I could see that his facial muscles were tense. I stopped the meditation and asked him what was happening. He then told me that the number *one* was the logo of his company and that thinking about it made him anxious over missed work, his illness, and many other things. So we chose a different focus, one that evoked a sense of peacefulness, and he was fine.

Some people prefer a neutral sound. For them the word *one* works fine. Sounds with *mmm* and *nnn* are traditionally used in meditation because they evoke pleasant associations like letting go and enjoyment. Other people prefer a phrase with meaning. *Peace*, *love*, and *let go* are common choices. Still others use a few words or a phrase from a prayer— either a familiar prayer or a prayer that comes spontaneously from the heart.

I often teach my patients to meditate when we are finished with their initial evaluation. It's always great to hear their choice of focus phrases and to have the opportunity to watch as they try them out. Each one has a different feeling and evokes a different mental set. One patient recently chose the focus "Dearest Lord" on the in breath and "I surrender to your grace" on the out breath. The peace that was generated as she meditated with that focus was palpable in the room. The power and beauty of her faith were magnified by making God her single focus. This is the reason for the religious use of meditation. Thoughts of God, when brought to the forefront, are much more powerful than when mixed into the background of daily concerns. The use of meditation in sports or creativity training is similar. The greatest connection to the task at hand can be made with a concentrated mind.

Eastern forms of meditation have traditionally employed focus words or phrases called mantras. A mantra is a word with spiritual meaning. For instance, the Sanskrit word *Om* has the same meaning as *the Word* in Christianity. It refers to the primordial sound, or vibration, from which the universe was created. Physicists might say it is the sound of the echo of the Big Bang. Neurophysiologists might say it is a good word for meditation because it entrains the mind in associations of pleasant things—*mmm* is the prototype of enjoyment.

The choice of a focus word is a matter for real contemplation. If you have religious beliefs, you might like to choose a word or phrase from your own tradition. If you do not, then choose something that evokes a sense of meaning that is important to you. This could be anything at all. One very tense patient chose a perfect focus to remind him of the shift in priorities that was a necessity for his health. His chosen focus was "My time."

If you cannot think of your own focus, you might want to try a very old Sanskrit mantra, *Ham Sah*. It is supposed to mimic the sound of the incoming and outgoing breath. It is called a natural mantra because it goes on day and night without stop. One needs only to tune into it. *Ham* means "I am" and *Sah* means "That." *That* is regarded as the part of the mind that witnesses all our experience—or awareness itself. We'll explore that topic in depth in Chapter 4. If you're religious, you can imagine this in-dwelling awareness to be your connection to God. If you're not religious, you can think of it just as awareness, as the power of the mind to overcome itself through the act of self-observation.

The Process of Meditation

1. **Choose a quiet spot where you will not be disturbed by other people or by the telephone.** This extends to animals as well. Inevitably, if you have a dog or a cat, it will find a way into your lap, so arrange to put it in another room.

Many of us are used to being at the beck and call of the world; this is one time you are not. *You must make time for yourself.* If you fail to make time for yourself, always putting other things first, you will never be happy, nor will you make others happy.

We have a rule about meditation in our house: Do not disturb unless there is blood involved. It's as simple as that. This is your time. Time you take for yourself to more fully understand the interaction of your mind, body, and spirit.

2. **Sit in a comfortable position,** with back straight and arms and legs uncrossed, unless you choose to sit cross-legged on a floor cushion.

3. **Close your eyes.** This makes it easier to concentrate.

4. **Relax your muscles sequentially from head to feet.** This step helps to break the connection between stressful thoughts and a tense body. For now, just become aware of each part of your body in succession, letting go as much as you can with the out breath. Take a second now just to take a deep breath in. Let it go. Notice how your body relaxes as you let go. This is the good old sigh of relief. The pull of gravity is always present, encouraging us to let go, but if there is no awareness of being uptight, there can't be any letting go. Notice your shoulders right now. Is there any room to let them down more, cooperating with gravity and your own out breath? Every out breath is an opportunity to let go.

Starting with your forehead, become aware of tension as you breathe in. Let go of any obvious tension as you breathe out. Go through the rest of your body in this way, proceeding down through your eyes, jaws, neck, shoulders, arms, hands, chest, upper back, middle back and midriff, lower back, belly, pelvis, buttocks, thighs, calves, and feet. This need only take a minute or two.

5. **Become aware of your breathing, noticing how the breath goes in and out, without trying to control it in any way.** You are breathing all the time, aware of it or not. You don't so much breathe, as you are automatically breathed. In the next chapter we'll take up breath control as a shortcut to eliciting the relaxation response. For the purpose of meditation, however, *let the breath happen by itself.* You may notice that your breathing gets slower and shallower as the meditation progresses. That's due to the physiological effects of the relaxation response, the fact that your body requires less oxygen because your metabolism has slowed down.

6. **Repeat your focus word silently in time to your breathing.** You may have chosen a word or phrase to repeat just on the out breath, or you may have a phrase that is broken up, part on the in breath and part on the out breath. In the case of *Ham Sah*, just listen to your breath, imagining that it sounds like *Ham* on the in breath and *Sah* on the out breath.

7. **Don't worry about how you are doing.** As soon as you start to worry about whether you are doing it right, you have shifted from meditation to anxiety. Without doubt, you will do this a lot at first; it's just the habit of the mind to question and criticize our own performance. If you notice that tendency, try labeling it *judging,* then let go, coming back to the breath and the focus, which are your anchors in the shifting tides of the mind.

Your mind will not stop for more than seconds at a time, if at all, so don't expect it to. What happens is that you, that part of yourself that can watch or witness the shenanigans of the mind, is learning to flex its muscles. Each time you notice that you've drifted into thought, try labeling where you were, for instance, *thinking, thinking* or *anger, anger* or *judging, judging* and then let it go, getting back to the anchor. In this way, you begin to train your mind in awareness—the antidote to denial and mental unconsciousness. The awareness you develop in meditation will begin to carry over into life, affording you much more choice in how you respond and restoring your ability to enjoy life. In meditation there are two basic choices, to keep observing the train of thought as a detached witness or to let go and come back to the breath. Inevitably, you will do both.

The most common experience and complaint about meditation is "I can't stop my mind from wandering." That's fine. Don't try. Just practice bringing it back to concentration on the breath and focus whenever you notice its wanderings. St. Francis had a great comment about wandering thoughts: You can't stop the birds from flying back and forth over your head, but you can stop them from nesting in your hair. Try to do just that. Let the thoughts come and go as if they were birds passing across the blue sky of a clear mind. The clear blue that you will perceive when the thoughts slow down is peace. Peace of mind.

8. **Practice at least once a day for ten to twenty minutes.** Remember that practice is indispensable to progress at anything. In meditation your goals are twofold. The session itself is the goal. In the true sense, the process is the product. Your only goal is to sit and do the meditation. Even if it seems that the only thing you're doing is chasing after your mind to tie it down again, remarkably the relaxation response is still most likely occurring. Long before patients think they know "how to do it," they begin to notice that they are generally feeling more peaceful and their symptoms are beginning to improve. The second goal is that, of course, it does get easier and more deeply peaceful after repeated practice.

If you can sit twice a day for ten to twenty minutes, so much the better. The preferred times are early morning, after a shower and exercise if you do it, but before breakfast, or before dinner. The only times to avoid are when you're tired, simply because meditation is a concentration exercise and, if you're tired, you'll fall asleep, and just after a heavy meal, since the process of digestion makes people sluggish.

☻ Reread the instructions and meditate for ten or twenty minutes before reading any further.

The Experience of Meditation

Beginning meditators have one or more of three basic experiences: relaxation, sleep, or anxiety. Let's take a close look at each of them as you review the experience of your own meditation.

Relaxation

Most people experience at least a few minutes of relaxation during meditation. It is easy to understand why. At those moments when the mind takes a back seat and the inner dialogue slows down, what is left is the experience of just being in the present. Even when that experience is simply watching the breath and repeating a focus, it brings about a sense of relaxation and peacefulness because that state is what our basic nature actually is. We experience peace whenever the mind slows down. Since we can't always participate in skiing, gardening, or whatever favorite activity slows our minds and thus gives us peace, meditation becomes a portable mini-vacation. It can always be experienced. As we'll see in the next chapters, meditation need not be confined to ten- or twenty-minute periods. It can be practiced for a minute or a few minutes anytime throughout the day. Furthermore, any activity can be engaged in as if it were meditation. *The final goal of meditation is to be constantly conscious of experience so that relaxation and peace of mind become the norm rather than the exception.*

Sleep or Drowsiness

Learning is a matter of association. When we close our eyes with the intent of letting go, sleep is the conditioned response that the body knows best. In fact, sleep cannot come until we let go, which is why worrying or excitement often result in insomnia. Therefore it is common to fall asleep or at least become drowsy when we first learn to meditate. The way to avoid this is to keep a straight back and not get too comfortable. Unless you have a physical problem that makes it impossible to meditate in a sitting position, don't meditate lying down. This will definitely invite sleep. With time, the body becomes reconditioned so that sleep is not an automatic response to letting go with closed eyes. It becomes easier to maintain a state of relaxed concentration.

If you have trouble falling asleep at night, however, then meditating while lying down is a great idea. Most people find that meditation is a big help to falling asleep and to sleeping more soundly. Even if you are generally asleep within minutes of hitting the pillow, it is a good idea always to meditate because sleep becomes much more restful.

The sleep state is variable. Everyone has had the experience of sleeping for eight hours and awakening completely rested on most occasions but exhausted on others. Part of the variation has to do with what happens during periods of rapid eye movement, or REM sleep, when you are dreaming.

Since the body cannot distinguish what is actually happening from what is imagined either during dreams or when awake, your body tells the tale of what happened in the dream state. If your dreams are restless, tense, or disturbing, they will affect how rested you feel upon awakening.

Never go to sleep listening to the radio or television. It's bad enough to have to contend with what your own mind manufactures without adding the negative fantasies of others picked up from television programs and particularly radio talk shows. As we'll discuss in Chapter 4, the conscious and unconscious minds are very close at the time of falling asleep, as they are during meditation, and you are particularly open to disturbing influences at those times. Protect yourself by going to sleep peacefully. If you must use the radio, listen to calming music.

If you awaken during the night, try meditating to fall back asleep. Counting sheep, you probably recognize by now, is a form of meditation. Meditating for regular periods during the day builds the mental muscles of letting go, making it is easier to call on them when you need to focus the mind and let go so that you can fall asleep. About half of the people who come to the Mind/Body Clinic have sleep disturbances. Either they have trouble falling asleep, trouble staying asleep, or they wake up too early in the morning and can't get back to sleep. A significant number of them find that they once again can sleep after several weeks of meditation practice.

If you are troubled by insomnia, there are a few hints to keep in mind. First, give up beverages containing caffeine. You may be surprised at the rapid improvement in sleep. Secondly, don't ever use alcoholic beverages to make you drowsy so that you can sleep. A few hours after a drink, there is a rebound phase of excitement of the sympathetic nervous system, very similar to a fight-or-flight response.

This shift in the nervous system often awakens people with a feeling of anxiety and restlessness. Thirdly, beware of sleeping pills beyond their use as a temporary measure for extreme stress. The body habituates quickly to most sleeping pills and requires progressively more of the same medication for the same results. The morning "hangover" disrupts the ability to concentrate and simply feeds the cycle of stress and tension that the pills were suppose to interrupt. If you are currently addicted to sleeping pills, consult your physician for a schedule of gradual withdrawal from the medication, substituting meditation. Fourthly, if you awaken in the night and are unable to get back to sleep within fifteen minutes, get up and meditate. This will convert useless time to a chance to rest very deeply. Some of the early experiments that Dr. Benson performed showed that the body's metabolism, as measured by oxygen consumption, drops further during a twenty-minute meditation than it does during eight hours of sleep. The restful, hypometabolic physiology of the relaxation response will substitute for some of the lost sleep, and you will feel much better the next day.

Catnappers may also find that ten to twenty minutes of meditation is a much better battery recharger than thirty to sixty minutes of napping. Try it out and see.

Anxiety

About one-third to one-half of all new meditators become anxious during some part of meditation. The reason is simple. Meditation is a time when you are left alone with your own mind. There are no distractions. All the worries that you may be trying to keep at bay by keeping busy have the opportunity to flood in and vie for your attention. I call this the anxiety parade. It may vary from the common "laundry list" experience of rerunning all the things you have to do, to the sudden realization of the things you haven't yet done—forgotten phone calls and the like—to more deep-seated problems.

If you take the position of observing the worries, as St. Francis suggested, just letting them come in and go out without grabbing on to them and letting them nest in your hair, then by and by they will wind down. Like an insistent child who tugs on your coattails for attention, your mind must be gently reminded that this is the time for letting go instead of holding on, and it will soon make the new association and slow down.

The most universal reason for experiencing anxiety during meditation is performance anxiety. Nearly everyone gets involved in deciding that they are doing it wrong. People worry over the tendency of the mind to wander, but nothing could be more natural that noticing the ongoing inner dialogue. *The primary goal of meditation is not relaxation—it is awareness. This is what leads eventually to getting the mind back under control. Relaxation is a side effect of learning how to meditate.* Therefore a restless meditation is usually a better learning experience than one where the mind becomes peaceful. In time the mind will slow down faster and faster as you build the facility of becoming aware and making the choice to let go.

Meditation is a form of mental martial arts. It's not that the mind stops attacking, but that we learn to take a different stance toward the attack. If you start to berate yourself for being restless, you have picked up the invitation of your mind to do battle, and battle is what you will experience as tension and anxiety. Instead, learn to adopt the stance of the karate student. Move gracefully aside and let the thoughts speed by without engaging them in a struggle. In that way, the mind will tire itself out as you hold the centered position of witnessing your own thoughts.

The process of meditation is similar to that of trying to balance your checkbook with the television turned on. At first you are into adding up the checks, concentrating on the task at hand. Then something loud occurs on the TV, maybe a commercial. For a moment it grabs your attention. You get involved in the show. Sooner or later you say, "Wait a minute, I'm supposed to be balancing my checkbook," and you let go of the TV and surrender once again to the checkbook. This dance of going back and forth may continue for quite some time. So it is with the process of meditation. When you finish balancing the books, you won't say, "What a lousy checkbook balancer I am—I keep getting distracted." Instead, it is more likely that you will be pleased at having completed the task. It's the same with meditation. *Remember, the only definition of a good meditation is one that you did.*

Since meditation is a process of awareness, you will become progressively more tuned in to what goes on in your mind. At times old memories and long-forgotten incidents may reveal themselves. Some of these may be disturbing. That is natural and good. Consider it analogous to how the body rids itself of a splinter. At first the splinter causes pain, but if it's too deep to remove, soon the body becomes insensitive to it. Similarly, when something painful happens that you can't work out at the time, the experience will recede deeper into your unconscious. This is the mechanism of denial. Sooner or later the body will mount a response to the splinter, and an irritation will develop around it and then an infection. The resulting infection will cause some pressure and pain, but in the process the buried splinter will be lifted to the surface and finally expelled. In meditation the splinters of the mind will also work themselves to the surface with time, where you become aware of them and can finally take action in resolving the cause of the discomfort. In some cases you will have to take some action as Nancy did in having to confront her alcoholic husband with real resolve. In other cases the action you take will be the act of letting go. In the succeeding chapters we will deal more with how to use the awareness that meditation creates.

🖎 *Suggestions for the Reader*

1. Meditate daily, once or preferably twice, for ten to twenty minutes each time. A kitchen timer is a good reminder, but don't startle yourself with a loud alarm.

2. Set aside a special place in your home for meditation. Remember, the mind learns by association. When you sit down at the dinner table, you probably experience hunger, salivation, and other eating-related responses before the meal actually comes. When you sit down in your TV chair, your mind immediately sinks into a receptive state of watching. When you enter your clothes closet, your "time-to-get-dressed" program takes over so that you can move efficiently. It's the same with meditation. The place where you habitually meditate takes on the energy of that activity. Many of my patients have commented that every time they pass their meditation place, they feel a sense of peacefulness and letting go even if they don't sit down at that time.

Your place of meditation can be any corner, or a room if you have the space, where you don't do anything else. Make it pleasing and restful. Some people enjoy decorating the area with special pictures or plants or objects that are meaningful. Your meditation chair or cushion is best reserved for only that activity. Since you will be sitting still for ten to twenty minutes, your position is very important. You should feel comfortable and well balanced. Soft chairs are generally the least comfortable because they provide inadequate support. A hard chair with a straight back will be the most comfortable kind of seat. You may place a cushion behind your lower back to keep your spine straight, which will help you sit comfortably and reduce the possibility that you will fall asleep.

Since you will be still for an extended period, you may start to feel chilly even though your skin temperature warms. Therefore it's good to have a sweater or shawl to wrap yourself in so that physical discomfort will be less likely to distract you. *Remember, this is time that you take for yourself. Let your family know that it is important to you and that you are not to be disturbed.*

3. Remember not to judge your performance. In fact, try not to judge anything in meditation. At its best, meditation is a state of nonjudgmental awareness. Let your judge and censor rest for a while. It's a real relief.

3

Breaking the Anxiety Cycle

Roger, a twenty-seven-year-old division manager for a high-tech firm, came to the Mind/Body Clinic with two related problems: high blood pressure and fear of public speaking. Roger's blood pressure had been elevated for about two years, almost precisely as long as he had worked in his current job. Labeled a "whiz kid," he had risen quickly through the managerial ranks, compulsively trying to stay in control of all possible situations.

He arrived ten minutes early for our first meeting. I had a brief errand to run and caught sight of him as I left my office. He was perched at the edge of his chair, his right leg bouncing up and down, while he quickly leafed through an article on the clinic. After a short delay in the medical records office, I was five minutes late for our appointment. Was he mad!

During the course of Roger's evaluation, he continued to play beat the clock. He was aggressive, often hostile and confrontational. Roger was so restless that he was in motion even while sitting; his leg bounced and he constantly shifted positions. He looked like a tiger ready to pounce. His bodily tension was mirrored by mental tension. Roger could think of six things at the same time—phone calls, dinner plans, appointments—and frequently tried to take care of them all at once—a trait known as polyphasic behavior.

Physiological research indicates that people like Roger—Type A personalities—have a more reactive sympathetic nervous system, the fight-or-flight system, than do Type B's. The heightened arousal of the sympathetic nervous system, when chronic, leads to increased serum cholesterol, blood pressure, and cardiac output, all of which increase the risk of coronary artery disease and heart attack. It's as if Type A's see almost any situation as a threat and so are constantly on the ready.

The most recent research on Type A behavior indicates that the hostility component has the strongest correlation with heart disease. In my session with Roger, he described how he had learned to keep his anger under wraps, restraining himself from chewing out others when they didn't do things exactly his way. He got similarly angry at anything that blocked his compulsive need to control things, like having to wait in line. Repressing anger is very dangerous to the body, however, since it results in elevated blood pressure and other damaging cardiovascular changes. Learning to deal with emotions, as we'll do in Chapter 7, was an important part of Roger's treatment, as was breaking the cycle of anxiety and impatience using the two techniques you'll learn in this chapter.

Roger told me frankly that he wanted to lower his blood pressure behaviorally so he could avoid medications, some of which can cause sexual dysfunction in males. Before his visit, he had already begun his own program for physical well-being. He had taken up jogging for cardiovascular exercise, reduced his salt intake, and lost ten pounds. What needed attention was his behavior. Roger's inner dialogue revolved around constant doubt of himself, to which he responded by trying to control every circumstance. Life was one big threat. This was the cause of his performance anxiety. He was almost phobic of speaking before an audience, an important part of his job. Roger would begin to worry about his presentation a week in advance, always awfulizing about its outcome. He fantasized that he would panic and become tongue-tied during his speech or during the question-and-answer period. He was terrified of not knowing an answer and of not being able to articulate what he wanted to say. His worst fear was being exposed as a fraud and losing his job. Roger carefully explained to me his behavior before a speech. His mouth became extremely dry, his palms became sweaty, his heart pounded, and he had a sinking sensation in his stomach. These anxiety cues became part of a feedback loop that made him even more anxious. His hands trembled and his chest muscles tightened, causing him discomfort. He would then start to wonder if he was having a heart attack, thus escalating the anxiety cycle into high gear.

Once you have begun to awfulize, engaging the fight-or-flight response, you tend to lose perspective. Instead of thinking about all his successful presentations, Roger dwelled only on disaster. He would lose control. This time he would be exposed. Once on track, the anxious mind does not deviate; it is hard to distract. One-track thinking is adaptive in cases where you are actually in an emergency situation and need full attention to escape. In situations that are only mentally threatening, however, this survival wiring becomes a trap. The worried mind engages the fight-or-flight circuits. The muscles tense up. The question for Roger, and any of us who become trapped by anxiety, is how to break the cycle.

Cutting Through the Anxiety Cycle

In Figure 1 you can review how anxious, awfulizing thoughts lead both to *visceral feedback* and to *musculoskeletal feedback*. Roger experienced anxiety both ways. Viscerally, he was aware of dry mouth, sweaty palms, and a racing heart, and he also felt a sinking sensation in the pit of his stomach. These were all feedback from his **autonomic nervous system.** When Roger perceived these symptoms, his mind interpreted them as threats, which, through fight-or-flight, increased his arousal level even more. This vicious cycle can culminate in complete helplessness if it escalates to panic. The attempt to stay in control leads paradoxically to exactly such a loss of control.

Roger's sense of losing control was amplified by the response of his **musculoskeletal system** to his awfulizing thoughts. Roger's chest was tense, and he could see his hands shaking. These cues also fed back to increase the speed of his thoughts, adding thoughts about whether he could have a heart attack or drop his papers.

Take a moment now and close your eyes. Recall a time when you felt anxious, allowing yourself to relive it in as much detail as you are comfortable with. See if you can tell whether you react predominately with physical tension or with autonomic arousal.

The two following cycle breakers will help you deal with the anxiety cycle.

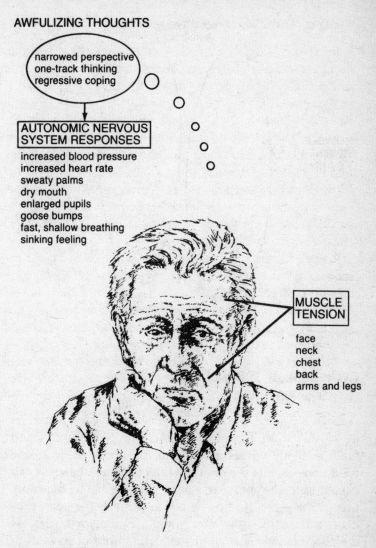

AWFULIZING THOUGHTS

narrowed perspective
one-track thinking
regressive coping

AUTONOMIC NERVOUS
SYSTEM RESPONSES

increased blood pressure
increased heart rate
sweaty palms
dry mouth
enlarged pupils
goose bumps
fast, shallow breathing
sinking feeling

MUSCLE
TENSION

face
neck
chest
back
arms and legs

Figure 1. The Anxiety Cycle

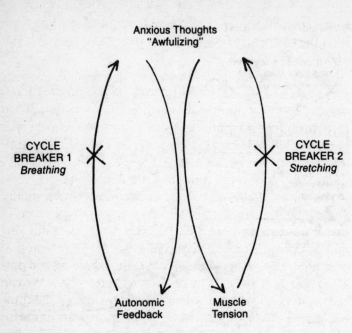

Figure 2. Cycle Breakers

Cycle Breaker 1: Breathing

An old fable concerns a poor man who, while wandering through the forest one day, discovers a dusty blue bottle. As he brushes it off, out pops a genie! The genie promises to fulfill as many wishes as the man can think of, with one condition—should the man run out of wishes, the genie can devour him. The poor man agrees, figuring that he can easily occupy the genie. His first wish is for a meal. The genie produces it instantly—row after row of steaming delicacies. As the poor man gazes at all this food, he thinks of servants to feed him. No sooner does this thought reach his consciousness than it is fulfilled. One wish follows another. Soon he is in a beautiful mansion with a charming wife and wonderful children. With difficulty, they keep the genie busy, but soon the man and his wife start to worry that they will run out of wishes.

The man remembers that a wise man lives in a hermitage about two hours distant. He and his wife hike to the hermitage in hopes that the wise man will have a solution that will save them from the genie. Indeed, he does. He tells the pair to erect a tall pole and tell the genie to keep busy by endlessly shinnying up and down the pole. If they need anything, they can just call him down for a moment.

The genie, of course, is a metaphor for our own minds. The minute the mind is not actively engaged, it threatens to eat us up with anxieties and negative fantasies. Shinnying up and down the pole is a metaphor for the breathing process. If the mind is kept busy noticing the incoming and outgoing breath, then it has no chance to overcome us. We can call on it as our servant rather than allowing it to become our master. This is the wisdom of all ancient and modern psychologies.

Breathing is an autonomic—or essentially automatic—bodily function that proceeds on its own but which we can also change voluntarily. While it is impossible to decide how fast we would like our hearts to beat, anyone can change the rhythm and depth of breathing. Changing breathing can, in turn, reduce or increase sympathetic nervous system activity, triggering either the fight-or-flight response or the relaxation response.

Learning to notice your breathing pattern and being able to change it from tension-producing to relaxation-producing is one of the most crucial—and simplest—mind/body skills. This skill interrupts the genie of the mind, which is sometimes all that is required to let go of anxiety-producing thoughts. (In other instances, it is important to examine the thoughts themselves—where they come from and how they can be changed. We'll explore that dimension in Chapters 5 and 6.)

The second of the ten weekly sessions of the Mind/Body Group is dedicated to breathing. Whether or not patients continue on with their meditation practice when the group is over, they all keep breathing. I get cards and calls from people years after they finish the program, thanking us again for the very simple tool of learning to breathe properly.

Abdominal Breathing: Relaxed Mode

If you have observed a baby breathing, you've had an excellent demonstration of proper technique. When a baby breathes in, you can watch how its abdomen expands like a balloon, and when it breathes out, you can see the abdomen flattening. When we fall asleep at night, exactly the same pattern occurs. In fact, whenever we're truly relaxed, the body reverts to abdominal breathing.

The diaphragm is a large sheet of muscle located right underneath the lungs, separating the lung cavity from the abdominal cavity. In Figure 3, you can see that it is shaped like an inverted bowl or dome. It contracts and moves down, flattening out during inhalation. Its downward movement creates a negative pressure in the lungs, and the lower lobes fill with air. Since its downward motion pushes on the organs within the abdominal cavity, the belly expands as the breath comes in. Exhalation is nothing more than a letting go. The diaphragm pops back up into its relaxed position, pushing the air out of the lungs. The belly then flattens back out. The bottom five pairs of ribs are called the floating ribs. They expand through the action of both the diaphragm and the intercostal (between ribs) muscles and fill the middle portion of the lungs after the lower lobes are filled by the action of the diaphragm. The last portion of the lungs to fill is the upper portion, ending just below the collarbone. In

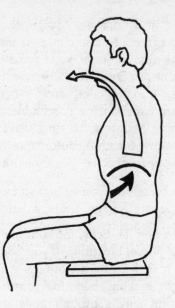

A. EXHALE
Diaphragm relaxes, pushing air out.
(Belly in)

B. INHALE
Diaphragm contracts, pulling air in.
(Belly out)

Figure 3. Abdominal Breathing

proper breathing, there is a complete exchange of air in the lower, middle, and upper portions of the lungs.

Unfortunately, once infancy passes and we begin to live in the fantasies of the mind more than the reality of the moment, the breathing pattern begins to shift as well, mirroring our various emotional states. Breathing is truly the mirror of the psyche. Recall for a moment the last time you were truly frightened. What happened to your breathing? Chances are that you either held your breath—breathing stopped altogether—or that your breathing became very fast and shallow.

In Figure 1 you can review the autonomic changes that occur with anxiety. Breathing is one of those changes, and sets the tone of the rest of the autonomic nervous system. Proper breathing is really a mini-relaxation response, creating almost identical physiology. It makes good sense. When the mind is at rest and we are experiencing peacefulness, breathing is relaxed. If the mind is stormy, creating waves that obscure peacefulness, restoring breathing automatically restores peace of mind. This is one feedback cycle that works to our advantage!

Chest Breathing: Tense Mode

The ideal of puffed-out chest and flat belly, for both men and women, is the antithesis of proper breathing. If you hold your belly in or if you force it in with tight clothing, you effectively freeze the diaphragm, making abdominal breathing impossible. The way to a trim belly is through moderate eating and appropriate exercise, not through holding your breath. In fact, when you learn to breathe properly, using the abdominal muscles, it will actually help to flatten your belly. As long as you hold the belly rigid, breathing can occur only in the upper portion of the chest. The typical chest breath moves only about 500 cubic centimeters of air— about half a pint. A full diaphragmatic or abdominal breath moves eight to ten times that volume!

You can probably appreciate how tiring the extra muscle activity is to breathe fast enough to move all that additional air with only the intercostal muscles. People who complain of fatigue are often amazed at the difference proper breathing can make. It not only eliminates the needless effort of chest breathing, but also supplies more oxygen for fuel. The brain is the organ with the greatest oxygen need, and you will notice a difference in your level of alertness immediately after just ten or so proper breaths. When you think about "brain food," the best fuel of all is oxygen, and the best way to deliver it in precisely the right quantity is through abdominal breathing.

Learning to Breathe

STEP 1: How am I breathing?

Since most of us are unaware of breathing, we have no chance to use it to our own advantage. In this exercise you will learn to identify abdominal and chest breathing so that you can learn to breathe properly.

Sit in a straight-backed chair and then slide forward a few inches so that you are reclining slightly. You can put a pillow behind your lower back if you like.

Place one hand palm down over your navel and place the other hand on top of it.

Without trying to change your breathing in any way, simply notice whether your belly is expanding or flattening as you inhale. It's easiest to do this if you close your eyes so that you can really concentrate.

Take a moment and try this now, noticing the next five breaths. If your belly expands as you breathe in, you are breathing at least in part from your diaphragm. If your belly doesn't move or goes flat as you inhale, you are breathing from your chest.

STEP 2: Shifting from chest to abdominal breathing

Take a deep breath in and then blow it out completely through your mouth, like an audible sigh of relief. As you do this, notice how your belly flattens, and flatten it even further, squeezing out every last bit of air. Now just let the next breath flow in by itself through your nose. Can you feel your belly expand? If not, try again.

The trick to shifting from chest to diaphragmatic breathing is to exhale completely for just one breath. This is why we exhale the one breath through the mouth—to fully evacuate the lungs. This full exhalation pushes out all the stale air from the bottom of the lungs, and the resulting vacuum automatically pulls in a deep, diaphragmatic breath. *You need to breathe out deeply only once or twice. Think of it as a sigh of relief.* Sighing and yawning both result in a deep air exchange and are the body's way of letting go of stress and tension.

Continue breathing through your nose, imagining that the incoming breath is filling a balloon in your belly. When your belly is full, let go and feel the balloon emptying as you exhale. Two or three minutes of abdominal breathing provide a real time out from tension. Even two or three breaths make a difference.

Practicing Abdominal Breathing

Whenever you get caught up in anxiety—worry and tension—you can break the cycle by shifting into abdominal breathing. Once you've mastered it, of course, you can keep your eyes open. It works anywhere and at any time. Standing in your kitchen, waiting in line, riding in an elevator, driving down the highway, you can always breathe.

Several years ago Myrin and I were at a scientific meeting where biofeedback equipment was being sold. (My own particular bias is that most people don't need the feedback from a machine to know that they're relaxing; it's easy enough to master on your own.) As a sales come-on, one manufacturer was using a biofeedback machine that monitored finger temperature to create a diabolical game—who could relax fastest. What happens when you play a game and win a point? You become excited, right? That turns on your autonomic nervous system, you get tense, then your hands get cold. The more relaxed, the warmer your hands and feet. My husband and I decided to give it a try. At first we were running at a dead heat. We'd each win a point, get excited, cool down, and lose the next. Then I remembered to breathe. I forgot the game, heaved a sigh of relief, shifted to abdominal breathing, and just concentrated on the rise and fall of my belly for the next minute. By the end of that time I'd won the game.

Remember, take a deep breath and let it go with a sigh of relief. Then feel the next several breaths entering the abdomen, letting it swell like a balloon on the in breath, letting go on the out breath.

The Ten-to-One Countdown

One excellent breathing technique combines abdominal breathing with meditation to produce a deep, quick change in physiology and attitude. Breathe in and let go with a sigh of relief to shift to abdominal breathing. Take another breath, and in your mind's eye watch it fill your belly. As you breathe out, silently repeat *ten*, letting go of tension as if it were a wave moving from your head, down your body, and out through the soles of your feet. Imagine the feeling of letting go. On the next breath, repeat the technique, counting *nine* on the out breath. On the eight subsequent breaths count back all the way down to *one*. Unlike Dr. Benson's experiment, where students lost count, here you're only counting down once and in one direction. If you do lose count, don't worry. Pick up wherever you think you are. *Take a moment and try this now before reading on.*

Notice how you are feeling? More relaxed, right? You may also observe that your breathing has slowed way down—a sign of the relaxation response. As you become more proficient with this technique through practice, you require shorter and shorter sessions because your nervous system has learned another beneficial conditioned response. Just two or three breaths will bring you the benefits of a longer period of meditation.

A Note to Hyperventilators

Some people become so anxious that they literally feel that they can't catch their breath and they are going to pass out. Contributing to this state of hyperarousal is a rapid heart beat. These bodily sensations feed back to the thought process and escalate the anxiety cycle to stunning proportions. Once in this state, a person may begin hyperventilating, breathing very rapidly, which further complicates matters by producing a sensation of light-headedness that reinforces the fear of losing control or passing out.

To cut through the cycle of hyperventilation, you have to behave counter-intuitively. When feeling as if you're about to suffocate, you try to get more and more air. The reason you cannot is that the lungs are already full. To break the cycle, concentrate on breathing out. It's the same technique we've been talking about. Breathe out a big sigh through your mouth, push out all the air, and in your mind's eye watch the in breath fill the belly. Then try the ten-to-one countdown.

Cycle Breaker 2: Stretching

After a few weeks of practice, Roger was able to use breathing to relax at home and work. Ten minutes before a talk, he would close his office door and do five minutes of abdominal breathing. As he walked to a conference room, he would breathe. As he got his slides in order, he would breathe. After about a month, Roger reported that meditation and breathing had reduced his performance anxiety to a manageable level. Although his blood pressure also had come down, he continued to feel fidgety and had difficulty sitting quietly. In anxiety-provoking situations, his breathing calmed his autonomic symptoms, but his chest was still tight. To relax the muscles, Roger had to learn to de-escalate the anxiety feedback loop.

In this next session I'm going to lead you through two brief body relaxations. The first is the Anytime Series. It takes just two to three minutes to complete and can be done in a chair at home, in the office, on the bus, or anyplace at all. The second is the Full-Body Relaxer Series, which requires fifteen to twenty minutes and a place large enough to stretch out on a rug or mat on the floor.

The Anytime Series

This series is composed of four exercises followed by the ten-to-one countdown. It is designed to relax tension as quickly and efficiently as possible in the major areas that people store tension: back, chest, shoulders, neck, and face.

All the exercises are based on the same principle. Various body parts are *tensed on the in breath* and *let go on the out breath*. Every out breath is an opportunity to let go. Before we begin, take a moment to notice your breathing. If it's in your chest, breathe a sigh of relief and watch your belly expand like a balloon on the next in breath. Now notice your torso. Your whole upper body rises up on the in breath and sinks back on the out breath, letting go to the pull of gravity.

The pull of gravity is a natural ally. Each out breath represents an opportunity to let go of any tension you may be holding. Gravity itself will pull your muscles back to their resting positions. We create an incredible amount of useless tension by opposing the pull of gravity and holding tension in body parts that aren't being used.

Find a chair in which you can sit comfortably. It's best for the chair to be hard because part of the exercises will require you to perch comfortably on its edge. The best way to learn these exercises is to read them through. Look at the sketches and imagine how each exercise will feel. Then read the directions into a tape recorder, slowly and soothingly, pausing as indicated for as long as you sense you will need. You can personalize the tape by recording simple and calming music in the background. If you do this, keep the volume of the music very low.

Sit comfortably in your chair with both feet on the floor and your arms resting easily on your lap. Close your eyes and breathe out the sigh of relief (pause), now breathe back abdominally from three to one (pause). Use every in breath as a moment of awareness to notice how much tension is in each body part. Use every out breath as an occasion to let the tension go. Notice your eyes. Let them soften. Now your jaws. Let your jaws relax as best you can. Become aware of your neck, let go with every out breath. Now your shoulders. Is there any room for them to drop further? Let your arms and hands rest heavily in your lap. Take a very deep breath and let your chest go. Your back, let it go. Feel your belly relax, expanding and contracting with the breath.

The four Anytime Exercises that follow will allow you to let go of even more tension. Make a note of where you feel residual tension now so that you can check your level of relaxation at the end.

EXERCISE 1: THE BACK RELAXER

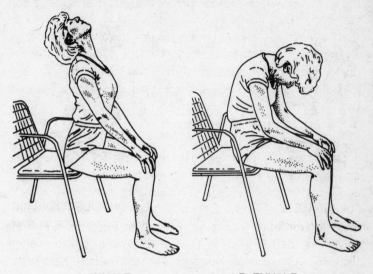

A. INHALE   B. EXHALE

Move to the edge of your chair. With eyes closed so that you can pay closer attention to inner sensations, notice how your back feels. On the next in breath, arch backward (**A**), stretching your spine only as far as feels comfortable. Exhale and round your back (**B**), rolling your shoulders forward and letting go. Repeat three times, keeping full attention on breathing, stretching, and letting go (long pause).

EXERCISE 2: SHOULDER SHRUGS

A. INHALE
Shoulders up

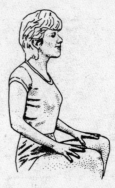

B. CONTINUE TO INHALE
Roll shoulder blades together

C. EXHALE
Shoulders down

Inhale and pull your shoulders up to your ears, (**A**). Now rotate your shoulders backward, pulling the shoulder blades together (**B**). Exhale with a sigh and let go (**C**). Repeat three times (long pause). Notice that when you pull your shoulder blades together, you are giving the chest muscles a nice stretch.

EXERCISE 3: HEAD ROLLS

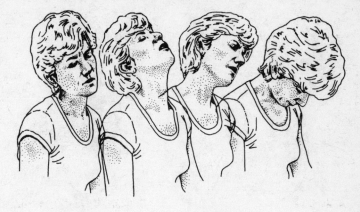

INHALE　　　　　　　**EXHALE**

Exhale as you drop your chin to your chest. Now inhale and rotate your head to the right, just letting it go, letting gravity take it rather than trying to push it around. When you have rotated your head around to the back, begin to exhale. Continue the exhalation as you roll to the left and back down to the chest. Now you're ready to inhale and start over. Complete three rolls to the right and then reverse, three to the left. Notice how the stretch moves around your neck as you do this? For instance, when you have dropped your head to the right, you can feel the stretch on the left side of your neck; when your head drops back, the stretch moves to your throat, and so on all the way around. Try to be aware of where you feel the stretch rather than where you are moving your head (long pause).

EXERCISE 4: FACE EXERCISES

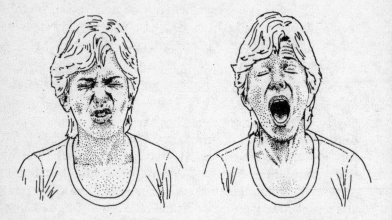

A. THE SCRUNCH
Inhale. Hold. Then exhale and let go.

B. THE YAWN
Inhale. Hold. Then exhale and let go.

The facial exercises are done in two steps. First, inhale and scrunch all your facial muscles in toward the center (**A**). It's as if you are trying to squeeze all the tension right off the tip of your nose. Exhale and let it go. Now inhale and open your mouth wide, lifting your eyebrows to make your face very long (**B**). This is like a yawn. When you exhale and let go, you may even find yourself yawning.

The Full-Body Relaxer Series

The following seven stretches were chosen to relax all the major muscle groups. In doing these exercises, keep two things firmly in mind.

1. These are gentle letting-go stretches. The best way to develop a supple, limber, and relaxed body is to focus on melting into each stretch. *Never bounce or push beyond what feels comfortable*. Bouncing defeats the purpose of stretching because the quick pull on the muscle fibers alerts special sensors within the muscle to the sudden overstretch. Nerve signals from those receptors then automatically shorten the muscle. Bouncing therefore causes muscle fibers to shorten and tense rather than lengthen and relax. Bouncing can also strain or tear muscles as you pull on a group of shortened muscle fibers.

2. If you have any physical problem that limits your ability to exercise, consult with your physician before doing these or any other exercises. You must take responsibility for knowing your own limits. Read each exercise through and study the diagram before you try it. As with the Anytime Series, taping the instructions for yourself is the best idea. Read the instructions very slowly into the tape recorder, trying to sense how long each movement will take you.

RELAXER 1: THE WALL HANG

Stand with your back to the wall, feet about shoulder width apart and nine to twelve inches out from the wall. Press the small of your back against the wall so that every vertebra is in contact with it. Close your eyes, breathe out a sigh of relief, and shift to abdominal breathing. Breathe slowly and naturally throughout this exercise. Begin by dropping your chin to your chest. Drop your shoulders and then peel your backbone off the wall, a single vertebra at a time if you can, continuing to drop forward. Your hips will slide up the wall as you drop down. When you have dropped as far as you can, just hang there. Let your head and shoulders go. Take three or four breaths as you hang loose (long pause). Now gradually come back up, trying to reattach your vertebrae to the wall, one at a time (long pause). When you get back up, lean against the wall, breathing abdominally, to rest. If you are breathing heavily, breathe through your mouth until you feel rested again.

Note: If you have any tendency toward back pain, bend your knees a little to avoid any strain on your lower back. Mention this at the very beginning of the taped instruction, just after the first sentence.

RELAXER 2: THE FOUNTAIN

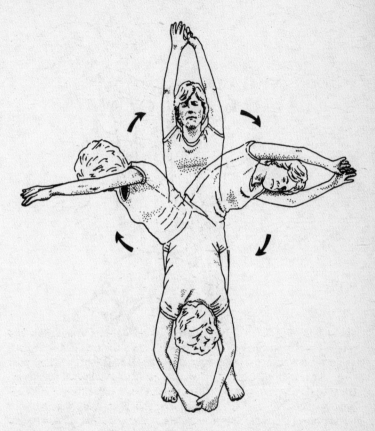

Stand with your legs about shoulder width apart. Inhale and stretch your arms *way up* over your head, locking your thumbs together, feeling the stretch along your sides. Exhale, circling to the right. Inhale and stretch way up again, exhale, and circle right. Go once more to the right and then reverse, three times to the left. Remember to just let go—there is no need to push or strain (long pause). Again, if you have any tendency toward back pain, bend your knees a little, inserting that direction after the first sentence.

RELAXER 3: THE CAT

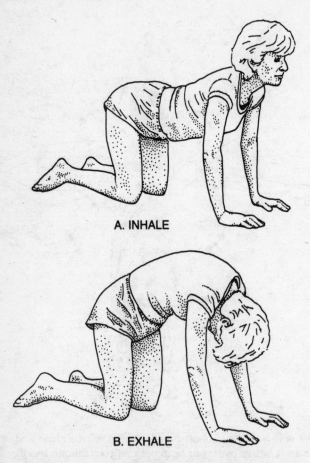

A. INHALE

B. EXHALE

Get down on all fours. Inhale, lifting your head up and pushing your spine down (**A**). Let your belly balloon out. Exhale, dropping your head and arching your back up like an angry cat, pulling in your abdominal muscles (**B**). Repeat three to five times (long pause).

RELAXER 4: LEG EXTENSIONS

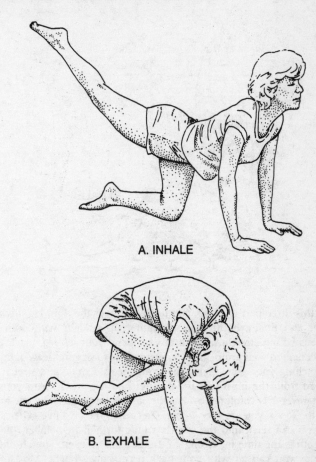

A. INHALE

B. EXHALE

Still on all fours, inhale as you lift your head up and extend your right leg out in back of you (**A**), toes pointed. Exhale, dropping your head down and bending your leg as you bring your knee toward your forehead (**B**). Repeat three times on the right side and three times on the left.

RELAXER 5: BENDING FORWARD

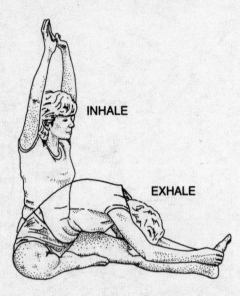

INHALE

EXHALE

In this three-part exercise, you bend first over the right leg, then the left, and finally both. Start by sitting up straight with both legs stretched out straight in front of you. Bend your left leg, placing the heel next to your groin, as if you were going to sit cross-legged. Inhale, stretching your arms high above your head. Exhale and stretch forward from the hips over the outstretched leg. Hold on to your leg wherever it is comforable—whether at the knee, the shin, the ankle, or the foot if you are very limber. On each of the next five exhales, see if you can relax into the stretch a little further. Remember, the out breath is the time for letting go. Don't push yourself. Stretch only as far as you can go with your back reasonably straight. Most of the power that helps you into this stretch comes from your abdominal muscles. See if you can use these to help you stretch forward (long pause). This stretch relaxes the hamstrings in the back of your legs and the muscles in the lower back. Repeat on the left side (long pause). Now stretch both legs out and repeat the stretch a last time (long pause).

RELAXER 6: PELVIC TILT

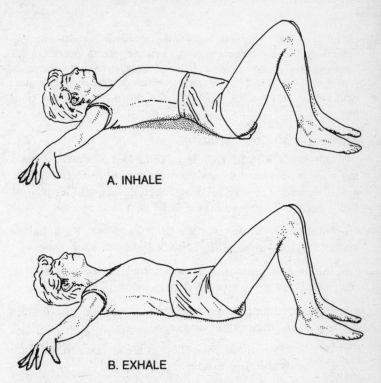

A. INHALE

B. EXHALE

Lie down on your back and bring your knees up so that your feet are close to your buttocks. Flatten your back down onto the floor by tilting your pelvis backward. Tilt your pelvis forward and let the space between the small of your back and the floor reappear. Now coordinate the movements with your breathing. Inhale as you rock the pelvis forward, making the space (A). Let your belly fill as you do this. Exhale as you rock backward, flattening your back against the floor (B). With a little practice, you will get the idea of pressing your vertebrae onto the floor one at a time and picking them off the floor in the same fashion. This is an excellent exercise for back tension. Repeat ten to twelve times (long pause).

RELAXER 7: FINAL RELAXATION

Lie on your back with your legs comfortably apart so that your toes point out gently toward either side. Let your arms rest a foot or so away from your body, and rotate your shoulder blades so that your palms turn gently up. Take five abdominal breaths, letting go a little more with each breath and letting yourself sink down into your mat (long pause).

Progressive Muscle Relaxation

1. Inhale and lift your right leg about a foot off the floor, making a fist with your toes and tensing as hard as feels comfortable. Hold for a few seconds and then exhale and let it drop. Roll your foot from side to side to let go a little more.

2. Inhale and lift and tense the left leg and foot. Hold. Exhale and let it go. Now roll your leg back and forth a few times.

3. Inhale and tense your buttocks, making them as hard as rocks. Hold for a few seconds then exhale and let go.

4. Inhale and puff out your belly as far as it will go. Hold for a few seconds, then exhale and let go.

5. Inhale and puff out your chest as far as you can. Hold for a few seconds and then exhale and let go.

6. Inhale, and lift your right arm off the mat, make a fist, and tense the arm. Hold for a few seconds then exhale and let go.

7. Inhale and lift yor left arm off the mat, make a fist, and tense the arm. Hold for a few seconds than exhale and let go.

8. Roll your head from side to side several times, breathing abdominally.

9. Inhale, scrunching your face toward the middle, then exhale and let go.

10. Inhale, making a yawning face with open mouth and raised eyebrows, then exhale and let go.

The Complete Breath

The perfect end to a period of relaxation is the complete breath. It is a variant of the abdominal breathing that you are already familiar with. Imagine that in place of your lungs there is a pear-shaped balloon with a long neck. The round part of the balloon is located in your belly, and the long neck extends up through the middle and upper chest. When you breathe in, imagine the belly expanding as the round part of the balloon fills. Then feel the neck of the balloon starting to fill as your middle chest expands. Finally, feel the top of the balloon filling you right up to the collarbone. As you exhale, feel the top of the balloon under the collarbone empty first, then feel the middle of the balloon emptying as your chest begins to flatten, and finally feel the round part of the balloon flatten as your belly shrinks back down toward the floor.

Take ten complete breaths, concentrating on feeling how the air fills the abdomen, the middle chest, and finally the top of the chest, and then noticing how it leaves the top of the chest, the middle, and finally the abdomen. This breath is particularly restful (long pause). It can be used not only at the end of a relaxation period, but like abdominal breathing, any time you need to break the anxiety cycle.

Breathing and Pain

Pain can be broken down into two parts. The first layer is the physical reality of the pain itself. The second added layer is the attitude we have about the pain. My migraines are an example. The pain was intense—throbbing pain that turned me nauseous at its crescendos—stabbing pain that made light intolerable. The second layer of the pain was the attitude that I added—the uncertainty about when the pain would pass, the impatience at being dragged out of my life and dropped into bed, the anger at my body's betrayal, the self-blame for being sickly, the helplessness and panic at being out of control, and the final layer of blame for letting things get so far out of hand. My body's response to that second layer was to get tense. Very tense. All my facial muscles tensed up around the headache and made the physical pain worse. In addition to the headache pain, the anxiety worsened the nausea and vomiting. This cycle of pain, anxiety–pain, escalates endlessly, making pain worse and worse.

The actual sensory experience of pain has a lot to do with attitude. A child who cut his leg while picking out his birthday present at the toy store would experience much less pain than the child who cut himself in math class. If the pain of childbirth were experienced after an automobile accident, the additional fear of the circumstance would render it completely unbearable. A friend of mine who is a gynecologist often explains it this way to her patients who suffer from premenstrual syndrome: "If you have a broken arm and life is going along fine, you hardly notice it. But if the boss is yelling and you're having a fight with your husband, the pain is a lot more disabling." Often she will send a PMS patient to the Mind/Body Clinic so that she can learn to change her attitude in a way that minimizes the PMS pain.

The most harmful attitude toward pain is to tense up around it physically or mentally, trying to push it away. All that resistance accomplishes is to increase the physical pain and the second, or added, layer of attitudinal discomfort. The premise we speak of again and again is *Whatever you resist persists.* The harder you try to escape, the more stuck you become. The big "reframe" in looking at pain is to accept it, relaxing around it physically and mentally. This means that you shift into the position of being an accepting observer of your pain rather than an unwilling victim. It doesn't require much thought to see that the observer has much more control than the victim. *To be in control of pain, you have to let go of trying to push it away.*

The next question is, what keeps you holding on? Sometimes it's lack of awareness. If you don't know that you've been holding on, then you can't let go. It's just like the ability to release tension in your shoulders as soon as you've taken a moment to observe that they're tense in the first place. Awareness of yourself, physically and mentally, is the first step.

A common reason for not wanting to let go of pain is that there is something that you need from it but think you cannot get any other way. Consider my migraines. My Type A behavior always caught me in the same bind. I would overcommit to the point where I knew it was impossible to get everything done, and then get increasingly tense and anxious. I would complain and blame others for putting me in a situation that I had obviously created myself. I would then become very fatigued, and sooner or later the headache would begin. The headache served several useful purposes. First, it showed those "insensitive" others whom I was blaming for my own overcommitment how mean they were and how much they hurt me. Second, it was the only legitimate way to get any rest and not have to produce for a while. A migraine headache takes precedence over anything that may need to be done. Third, it was the only way my body knew to release all the tension I had stored. A migraine always felt like a storm to me. When it was over, I lay limp, washed clean, and totally relaxed. Too bad that my body had to fight itself to death and then lie exhausted in order to let go.

Many of us do the same thing with pain and other illnesses and anxieties. Psychologists call these benefits of illness secondary gain. Why would I want to let go of the migraines? I needed them. As big as the price was, in the economy of my mind/body, clearly the migraines were worthwhile. The mind/body has incredible wisdom. It will seek whatever way it can, at the least possible cost, to bring us into a state of regulation.

We have tremendous power to change this balance through the use of awareness and breathing, choosing much less costly and more growth-productive ways of getting our needs met. Identifying whatever you might be getting as secondary benefits has to be done before you will be able to let go. You will then have to find healthy ways to get your needs met.

Using the Breath to Let Go of Pain

Close your eyes, center yourself with a sigh of relief, and shift to abdominal breathing. As you breathe, let yourself be fully aware of the pain. This may be physical pain or emotional pain like anxiety, guilt, fear, sadness, or depression that settles in your heart, belly, throat, or muscles. *Don't close off.* Open up to the pain. Pain is always moving and changing. At first, as you dare to notice it fully, it may seem more intense. Then it may flicker off and on or change positions. A pain can transform into heat or an electrical feeling, or it can transform into pleasure since the two sensations are actually close from a neuroanatomical perspective. Keep breathing abdominally and "watching" the pain, observing it with all your inner senses.

Now imagine that you can breathe in and out of the pain just as you can imagine breathing in and out of your belly. Imagine the in breath as loving attention—the opposite of trying to push away. It helps to support your imagination by recalling or imagining a time that you were really loved or loving. I always use a memory of breast-feeding one of my boys, rocking in a chair and cuddling the totally relaxed, content baby. You can feel the body's response to love in such a memory; it is an expansive, open, letting-go kind of feeling. As you breathe in, let that feeling of love penetrate the pain. Cradle it as you would a child. Breathe out and use your imagination to support the breaking up and flowing away of the pain. *Breathe and imagine without attachment to the results.* If you take a breath or two and then immediately begin to judge the results, you will soon be uptight again. Breathe and try to stay in the attitude of observation rather than judgment.

Mindfulness training was first introduced into behavioral medicine by Jon Kabat-Zinn, Ph.D., of the University of Massachusetts Medical School, who noted that this central component of Buddhist meditation practice was described traditionally as leading to the relief of pain and suffering. In a recent study of 225 chronic pain patients trained in mindfulness meditation techniques, which included stretching and breathing, he found that most patients continued to practice one or more of the techniques, and particularly the mindful breathing, for up to four years following their training. The large majority reported lasting moderate to great improvement in their pain over this time period. The suggestions for practicing mindfulness in daily life that are given in the next chapter are based on Dr. Kabat-Zinn's work.

✿ *Suggestions for the Reader*

1. Observe how you react to anxiety-provoking situations this week. Are you primarily an autonomic reactor or a muscular-tension reactor? Make note of this. Perhaps you respond in different ways to different hassles.

2. Practice abdominal breathing several times daily. Put up little signs where you will see them as reminders.

3. Practice the Anytime Series whenever and wherever you feel tension. You need not do the body-awareness exercise first unless you feel like it. The time to do it is when you feel you don't have the time, perhaps when you're tense and rushed and have a headache coming on. It takes only a few minutes but will save you many more by allowing you to carry on in a more relaxed manner. This series is great preventive medicine. Letting go of tension before your muscles set into concrete is much better than ending up with a headache, muscle spasm, or tension that requires aspirin or muscle relaxants to let go of.

4. Practice the Full-Body Relaxer Series once a day until you master it. You can then use the whole series or any part of the series when needed, although a daily regimen is preferred. The progressive muscle relaxation and complete breathing can be used anytime and is great in bed if you're having trouble falling asleep.

5. The complete breath can be used alone anytime. While it is easier to do initially while lying down, with experience you will also be able to do it sitting up.

6. For most people, the best way to learn effective stretching coupled with breathing is to look for a community class in hatha yoga. Yoga classes vary. Some are oriented entirely toward stretching, while others may incorporate a spiritual component. Be sure to choose the kind of class that suits you.

7. If you are working with a pain problem, consider what your secondary gains might be. Write them down and consider more healthy ways that you might get your needs met.

4

Mindfulness and the Discovery of the Self

Anyone who has ever sat at home, healthy, well fed, surrounded by loved ones, and suffering from intense anxiety will readily agree that peace of mind is the necessary condition for happiness. But how can we possibly learn to have peace of mind when the mind is by nature restless, projecting its wants and fears endlessly into the past and the future?

Think about your favorite activity for a moment. When you are really enjoying something you like, how do you feel? As you listen to your favorite music with full attention, other thoughts and desires fade away. You are simply in the moment. There is contentment—peace. Inevitably, of course, your mind kicks back in. How can you sit and listen to music? You need to clean the house, or think about your job, or get something to eat, or worry about finances, or make a phone call, or any of a thousand things. No longer in the moment, you're off and running.

If you could train your mind to let go of other desires, returning to them when the actual moment has come to do the bills and make the phone call, you would be able to experience peace of mind. The road to peace of mind is through a practice called *mindfulness*. Its opposite, the state in which the mind is in many places at once, is called *mindlessness*.

Alice Adelman Lowenstein, the real name of a brave and courageous woman, is a poet and fiction writer in her mid-forties. She was a member of the very first Mind/Body Group. Suffering from severe allergies, she could be laid up with debilitating dizziness by such seemingly innocuous events as a whiff of perfume or an unexpected ingredient in a meal. Alice found that several long periods of meditation during the day helped her allergies. She became a serious student of mindfulness meditation. This meditative practice consists of anchoring attention in the breath and then passively observing thoughts, feelings, perceptions, and sensations without judgment. Ideas of good and bad fade away and there is only a contented openness to the present.

Almost a year ago, Alice was in a near-fatal car crash. Her chest was crushed and her brain damaged when the car her husband was driving spun out of control on an icy road. Alice was given a 1 percent chance to live. Her recovery process was truly remarkable. After several weeks in the intensive care unit, Alice was moved to a rehabilitation hospital. Her entire vocabulary consisted of a few hundred words. Like some stroke patients, she had lost access to language. I can hardly begin to imagine the frustration for anyone, let alone for such a wonderful writer. Alice had also lost the ability to control her body. She was like a toddler who had to relearn the most basic skills of language and locomotion.

Alice smiled at me as she recalled the process of relearning how to walk. Each step was a meditation. Her entire concentration had to be riveted on the minutest sensations of walking; otherwise she would fall. When talking, she had to give full attention to stringing the words into a sentence. When playing with blocks to recover spatial skills, she had to perform every motion with complete awareness, with full attention. Every digression into mindlessness was obvious, since she could no longer perform the task. Normally, we have little awareness of where the mind is. Alice viewed this quick "feedback" system as a gift. Her disabilities became powerful teachers of how to live in the moment.

Mindfulness: Meditation in Action

Mindfulness is meditation in action and involves a "be here now" approach that allows life to unfold without the limitation of prejudgment. It means being open to an awareness of the moment as it is and to what the moment could hold. It is a relaxed state of attentiveness to both the inner world of thoughts and feelings and the outer world of actions and perceptions.

Mindfulness means really being present with the food when eating, enjoying it rather than thinking about other things. Mindfulness means openness to the experience of motion when taking a walk, and to the sights, sounds, and smells around you. During a full-day session that occurs at the midpoint of the Mind/Body Program, we take a long walk in a park by a river near the hospital. There is no "purpose" to the walk—nowhere to go and nothing to accomplish. The accomplishment is being present in the process of walking. Our patients are usually amazed at how incredible the commonplace is. They hear sounds and see sights with new ears and eyes, with the kind of enjoyment a child experiences.

Watch small children at play to see mindfulness in action. They may be playing with a simple object like a bowl. To an adult, the bowl is a container and it belongs in such-and-such a cabinet. To a child, the bowl has no limits. Turned upside down, it is a drum. Turned on its side, it is a wheel.

In fantasy it can become a cradle or a bucket or a space ship to the moon. To a child, everything is fresh and new. The more we think we know it all, the more closed off from the changing experience of life we become.

Mindfulness requires a change in attitude. The joy is not in finishing an activity—the joy is in doing it. Those of you who are Type A's will find that this is completely foreign to your usual way of perceiving things. Remember that Type A's tend to engage in polyphasic behaviors—they try to do several things simultaneously. The reality of thinking and doing, however, is that we can only think or do one thing at a time. The mind can dart back and forth between several things, but it can hold only one thing in full focus. Polyphasic thinking, therefore, actually wastes time. It also creates enormous stress. Mindfulness is well summed up in this story told by Nossrat Peseschkian:

> While on a trip, Abdu'l-Bahá, the son of Bahá 'u' lláh, the founder of the Bahá'i religion, had been invited to dinner with a family. The wife had good intentions and wanted to show her great culinary artistry. When she brought out the food, she apologized for the fact that it was burned. While cooking it, she had been reading prayers in the hope that the meal would be especially successful. Abdu'l-Bahá answered with a friendly smile and said, "It's good that you pray. But next time you're in the kitchen, pray from a cookbook."

Mindfulness to the task would have been a truer act of devotion than fragmenting the activities of cooking and praying so that neither one was well accomplished.

An Exercise in Mindfulness
STEP 1: Daily Mindfulness Exercise
In the Mind/Body Group, patients practice mindfulness each day. They choose an activity, whether brushing their teeth, toweling off after a shower, eating a piece of fruit,

making love—literally any activity at all—and they do it like a meditation. Mindfully. Try it. You will be amazed at how different a plum tastes when you are mindful.

STEP 2: Opening to the Moment

You can train yourself to be mindful by cultivating awareness of where your mind is and then making a choice about where you want it to be. For example, if you need the time walking to the bus stop to plan the day, then you have made a conscious choice. Try to plan without falling into rumination that leads to nothing but tension.

If you don't need to plan, then *just be*. Center on your breathing, let out a sigh of relief, and then let yourself experience the rhythm of breathing and walking. After a while you'll fall into a comfortable stride, perhaps two steps to the inbreath and two steps to the outbreath, or any cadence that suits you. This can be the focus—the anchor—that holds your mind still as you open up your attention to what is around you—the trees, the clouds, the people—without judging. Just enjoy the moment.

STEP 3: Awareness of Thought and Physical Reaction

Inevitably, while practicing mindfulness, your mind will wander. Learning to observe where it wanders to is also a practice in awareness. In the last chapter, we began training mindfulness at the most basic levels: the muscles and the autonomic nervous system. Here we become observant of the thoughts that produce these bodily changes. Thoughts are of two varieties:

● Nonafflicting: Thoughts like "I wonder what's for dinner?" or "Should I watch TV or read a book?" come and go all the time without getting a rise out of the body. They don't matter that much.

- Afflicting: Thoughts like "I wonder why my spouse and I don't get along?" or "I'm scared that my disease is going to kill me" get a definite rise out of the body. They produce an emotional response like fear, guilt, or anger. Because such thoughts draw us out of the present moment, as well as getting stored in the body, they are very powerful.

One of my patients, a young nurse who experienced anxiety attacks, was amazed when she realized that the anxiety did not spring full-blown from nowhere. There were certain thoughts that always preceded her attacks while others kept them going. When she learned to control her thoughts, her anxiety disappeared. As you'll see in the next chapters, it is possible to break the cycle of mindlessness, worry, and past conditioning at many places—thoughts, feelings, or action itself. Let's begin by considering how the mind acquires the conditioned habits that give rise to mindless repetition.

Mental Conditioning

Human learning is a process of conditioning. Once a certain event has occurred, mental impressions are formed that favor its recurrence under similar circumstances. Remember Pavlov's dogs? Emotional events are conditioned in a similar fashion. Like old tapes, stored impressions can replay endlessly throughout life. This mindless repetition continues unless we shine the light of awareness on them and change our past conditioning—erase the worn-out tapes.

When I was six, I was out walking with my father and a huge black dog came around the corner. My father panicked and immediately pulled me across the street. I was amazed at his fear, since the dog seemed so nice and I had wanted to pet him. The reality of the animal had very little bearing on our quite different reactions—on the thoughts produced by our minds.

My father's mother had been bitten by a dog when he was a child, and he had a powerful stored impression—a memory—that dogs are frightening and dangerous. I, on the other hand, had been around a wonderfully friendly collie that belonged to my good friend Nancy. My fondest wish was for a dog like hers. We rarely see things for what they are. Instead, we see the reflection of our own conditioning. We believe and act on opinions and assumptions as if they were reality, closing off other experiences. My father was prejudiced against dogs, and this attitude imprisoned him in an apartment for years, since he feared buying a house where there might be big dogs in the neighborhood.

Old tapes create walls of many types. Some, like the fear of dogs, are obvious. Others are more subtle. Sometimes, just the conscious awareness of an old pattern is enough to change the situation. Other times, it is just a start.

Ben was a fifty-eight-year-old plumber who came to me with chest pains and insomnia. Almost as an aside, he told me that he had a driving phobia. He could drive during the day, but not at night. He could drive east on the Massachusetts Turnpike, but not west. His phobia had begun about five years earlier, after he recuperated from head injuries that had left him with no memory of how they had occurred.

The usual treatment for a phobia is to get the person into a relaxed state and then help him or her imagine progressively more fear-producing renditions of the phobia while maintaining a state of relaxation. When the person can remain relaxed while the mind reruns the fearful fantasy, the conditioned response that leads to the anxiety cycle is broken. The fight-or-flight response is uncoupled from the mind's fantasies. I made a plan to see Ben during the sixth week of the Mind/Body Group, after he'd had time to learn to elicit the relaxation response. We would then go through desensitization, rewiring his fears to a state of relaxation.

At that time we constructed a hierarchy, or graded series, of situations that he found threatening. The least threatening was driving in the late afternoon. The most threatening was driving in the dark, west on the turnpike. Ben easily slipped into a meditative state and went through the first rungs of the hierarchy with no problem. Although his mind reran danger, he could allow his body to relax. I was thinking how easy this would be for him. He could replay the tape of the session a few times and then start by driving with his wife at night until in a few weeks he would be able to drive west on the turnpike alone. We were just approaching that step of the hierarchy when my fantasizing over how easy this would be evaporated.

Ben began to shriek. I put my hand on his shoulder, telling him that he could breathe and let go or breathe and complete whatever was happening inside. After a minute or two, Ben slowly opened his eyes. He shook his head, almost in disbelief: "That was an amazing experience. I can hardly believe it. It was as real as if it were actually happening."

Ben explained the memory that had made him shriek. One evening before Christmas about five years before, he got into his car and headed west on the turnpike. Suddenly he felt a gun barrel on the back of his neck. There were two men in the back seat. They ordered him to pull over to an exit and drive to a big field, where they robbed him. Ben woke up in the hospital with a severe concussion and with no memory of what had happened.

In the relaxed state of meditation, where the unconscious mind became accessible, his repressed memory had returned. For Ben, understanding the root of the phobia was a breakthrough. He could deal with the reality of what had caused it much better than with its shadow—the pervasive anxiety and chest pain that had left him sleepless for no apparent reason. His chest pain disappeared almost immediately, as did the insomnia, and over the next few weeks he regained his ability to drive as before, using breathing as a tool to let go and stay relaxed, countering his conditioned fear.

The fears that burn the old tapes into our memories may once have been real: The dog did bite, your parents were critical, or the robbers did attack. But to go on protecting ourselves once the situation has passed and, worse, to see the old situation where it doesn't exist are equivalent to building a prison and then volunteering to live in it. This kind of transferred fear is no longer useful and can destroy our health and happiness.

The mind is like the motor of a car. Its running provides the power necessary to move. When the mind is in gear, we are carried along by its power. Angry thoughts beget further angry thoughts. Fearful thoughts gather more fear to them, and the mind takes the form of whatever it becomes absorbed in. By shifting into neutral, taking a breath and adopting the position of the mindful observer, you can detach yourself from the mind even though it is still running. In this way the mind can ultimately become the servant rather than the master, if you learn to live in the present rather than the past or the future. In order to do this, it is necessary to appreciate how the mind functions.

The Mind as an Instrument

In the chapters that follow, we'll be dealing with various approaches to awareness and control of the mind. First, it is necessary to appreciate what the mind is and how it works. Throughout the ages, various philosophers and psychologists have developed different maps of the mind. The most sophisticated maps have arisen from long studies of meditation, since meditation is a microscope through which the mind can be observed and analyzed. Not surprisingly, the maps generated by meditative observation are similar to those of psychologists who get their data from studying common patterns of the mind in mental health and mental illness.

The usefulness of understanding the mind as a four-part psychic instrument is that it puts the mind in its proper place. *The mind is a tool we use; it is not meant to be our jailer.* Here is a mind map that can help you understand and use your mind to its best advantage:

1. **The conscious mind.** You can think of the most basic consciousness as sense perception. Before you start to make inner comments and value judgments about things, first you must perceive them. The sights, sounds, smells, tastes, and touches that our senses take in are the simplest forms of data we have about the world. At this level, a black dog is a black dog. It is neither scary nor pleasant. It just is. When we are babies, before we develop experience and language, sense perception is our primary consciousness.

2. **The unconscious mind.** Every one of our experiences is encoded as an impression within the nervous system. That's why we don't have to relearn to drive a car every time we get behind the wheel. As we'll see in Chapter 6, the unconscious is a treasure trove of learning that can be drawn on to bring wisdom to any situation. As we've already seen, it is also a Pandora's box of fears, disappointments, and old tapes that may no longer be relevant, yet persist.

3. **The intellect.** This is the capacity to reason, using data both from conscious sense perceptions and from stored learnings in the unconscious. The purest form of intellect is

"thinking by choice" rather than being trapped in unbidden rumination over "what ifs" and "if onlys." When the intellect is functioning clearly, unclouded by the fear and doubt of old tapes, the mind is in its glory, sensing new perceptions and creating new meanings.

4. **The ego.** This is the collection of opinions that we have about ourselves—the way we would describe ourselves to the world. It's an identity we have created for ourselves in order to feel safe and secure. Like a mask put on for the world, it protects against our conditioned fears. At some point, however, the ego's walls create more pain than they ward off. Personal growth requires first forming an ego, then understanding it, and finally transcending it.

The four parts of the mind will be dealt with further in the chapters that follow. Since the ego is the part of the mind that plays on conscious and unconscious fears, supporting mindless repetition of old mental tapes, it is important to understand its development so that it can be let go of, allowing mindfulness to express itself.

Development of the Ego: The Judge

The ego develops during childhood. At first the baby thinks that it is one with its mother. Later it begins to develop the sense of a separate self. If you've ever thrown up your hands in exasperation at the *no*'s of a two-year-old, you've seen the ego developing. All human beings need to know that they are persons in their own right, with their own needs and thoughts, capable of creating meanings that are uniquely theirs.

The basic role of the ego is to provide our own uniqueness with an identity through which to express itself. Unfortunately, the developing ego usually encounters a host of mixed messages that leave impressions of danger and insecurity. The child whose parents are too stressed or ignorant to provide adequate love develops various means of getting attention. These may range from being exemplary in every way to acting out by setting fire to the house. Both behaviors are simply attempts to get what the child needs in order to survive.

For most of us, the ego is a combination of impressions. It contains some behaviors that lead to intimacy, productivity, and creativity. It contains others that can be thought of as a collection of walls, erected to keep out hurts and seal in security. The biggest and saddest wall that many people erect is around their heart. Fearing hurt and abandonment, they close themselves off from love.

The ego expresses its insecurities by judging everything, trying to ensure happiness by keeping everything tightly controlled. For this reason I call the ego the Judge. It splits life into two rigid categories, good and bad. Blindly seeking good and avoiding bad, it is caught in the illusion that it must be good in order to ensure its own existence.

Eastern psychologies, based on the experience of observing the mind's habits, counsel that the work of an adult is to dismantle the ego—to break down the outdated walls of fear and insecurity that fuel the various acts and postures we adopt to appear acceptable. The ego is often compared to a mask that we put on to show the world and gradually become unaware of. We think it is who we are.

It is easy to recognize the ego's mask—its walls that keep out the illusion of pain. The Judge has one primary motive—to seek pleasure and avoid pain. From childhood, we are conditioned to equate security and pleasure with being good, and fear and danger with being bad. Since so many people harbor secret fears of being deficient in some way or not being good enough, it's no wonder that anxiety is rampant. In the deepest recesses of the unconscious, being bad threatens our very survival, bringing up primitive fears of abandonment and desolation. On all of the ego's walls, in their countless variations, is embroidered *survival*. I once heard someone say, "Excuse me for being alive." That comment runs deep; the notion that we must justify ourselves to have a right to exist is at the heart of fear.

All children want to be recognized for their accomplishments, and they want to escape criticism. Psychologists have learned an interesting thing about shaping or conditioning behavior. It's easy to condition behavior with positive reinforcement. If each small step toward a goal is praised, learning proceeds quickly. Punishment, whether verbal criticism or corporal punishment, also changes behavior, but not always in the direction that is wanted.

Our own behavior and the thoughts that support it are a convoluted mixture of responses to positive and negative reinforcement. Most people will go to any length to be right—to be perceived as being good. This can take the form either of being a compulsive perfectionist or of actually doing a sloppy job but blaming other people for lack of results. If you listen closely to your inner dialogue, you may notice that its main topic is about good, bad, or indifferent. You may clean the house and begin ruminating over whether other people will notice your good work and praise you. If you fantasize that they won't, they become bad and you become mad. Ever notice how critical adolescents are? They want things to be familiar. Strange things—people from other countries, new foods, strangers—are all potential threats. Long after we have developed the discrimination to tell a threat from a new situation, the relentless inner Judge stays hard at work, trying to keep us safe and keep us loved by being good.

Going Beyond the Mind: The Witness

A baby's mind has not yet developed. It has consciousness—that is, sense perception—but attaches no meaning to perception at first. Through experience and conditioning, the other three parts of the mind are built up. Out of what is the mind built? Do you cease to exist if your mind is entirely still, no longer functioning?

Try this experiment before reading further. Since the mind speaks in words, for the next minute become the witness, the listener of your mind. Close your eyes, breath a sigh of relief, take three abdominal breaths, and listen to your mind for one minute.

What happened? You probably had one of two experiences. Either you watched your thoughts go by or, strangely, there were no thoughts at all. My patients are often amazed that when they watch the mind closely, it tends to stop or slow down. Steve Maurer, my colleague at the Mind/Body Clinic, often says that the mind becomes embarrassed when we watch it. Usually the experience of witnessing the mind—whether the mind falls silent or keeps on running—is one of peacefulness. You don't stop existing if the mind becomes quiet. You are still aware of your own existence and your own consciousness, and that awareness is quite peaceful. Try the experiment again for a minute.

Meditation develops the ability to become aware of a completely nonjudgmental part of the mind, that of the Witness. The Witness is the part of your mind that watches—that is aware of thinking. Since the Witness is beyond the ego, it is not caught up in judging and is thus content in any situation. Another name for the Witness is the Self, or the unconditioned mind. It is the same in everyone because it is not conditional on what our experiences have been. It exists previous to experience and the arising of the different parts of the mind. In many different psychologies and philosophies, the ego is called the self with a small *s* because it represents our own personal history, complete with all the limitations of our attitudes and fears. The Self with a big *S* represents completely unlimited potential.

The recognition that there is an essential similarity in every human being—that the core of each of us consists of the same consciousness—is at the heart of most spiritual systems. Eastern philosophies talk of transcending the limitations of the ego so that the Inner Self can be recognized as part of the whole divine consciousness. Jesus, too, instructs us to love our neighbors as ourselves.

Many systems of psychological growth have a similar end point. When doubt and fear are dismantled, a person can become aware of an inner wellspring of security, compassion, peace, and joy that fuels his contribution to the wholeness of life, that allows him to realize or to actualize the potential that dwells within. The terms *self-realization* and *self-actualization* refer to the process that ensues when a person identifies with the Self or Witness rather than the ego.

Jon Kabat-Zinn likes to tell the story of a rabbi who once wrote to Albert Einstein in a moment of great personal distress. The man had two daughters, eighteen and sixteen. When the younger of them died, he couldn't comfort his remaining child. Einstein's reply is a moving summary of what spiritual and some psychological systems have identified as the process of personal growth.

A human being is part of the whole, called by us "Universe," a part limited in time and space. He experiences himself, his thoughts and feelings as something separate from the rest— a kind of optical delusion of his consciousness. This delusion is a kind of prison for us, restricting us to our personal desires and to affection for a few persons nearest to us. Our task must be to free ourselves from this prison by widening our circle of compassion to embrace all living creatures and the whole of nature in its beauty. Nobody is able to achieve this completely, but the striving for such achievement is in itself a part of the liberation and a foundation for inner security.

Most of us have had some experience of the Inner Self and its connection to a larger wholeness, even though we may not have thought about it in just that way. The memory of nursing my son, feeling completely at one with him, enveloped in love and peace, was an experience of the Self.

One of our cancer patients named Mary told her group a beautiful story of a very different but essentially similar experience. Mary had known about her ovarian cancer for just a few months and, having completed surgery, was midway into a short course of chemotherapy. She and her husband decided to drive to the Adirondack Mountains to rest from the strain of the previous months. They were sitting by a clear mountain lake on an early spring day in the late afternoon, listening mindfully to the songs of the birds and the sounds of the wind. The setting sun was fanning out into a mosaic of reds and blues that shimmered as it reflected on the still surface of the water. Suddenly, Mary lost the usual perception of herself looking *at* the water. Instead she felt a powerful experience of being at *one* with the water, the birds, the sky, the earth, and her husband. The boundaries between herself and her perceptions had melted away. Later Mary realized that the experience had lasted for about ten minutes, but it had seemed timeless.

Struggling to put her emotional state into words, Mary focused on transcendent peace, at-one-ment with the universe, and total love. She went on to say that she now felt less fearful about the cancer because she had experienced firsthand that human consciousness was not limited to the individual. The other group members were quite moved by her description, which triggered memories of similar, though less intense, experiences they had had at different times in their lives.

Even-Mindedness: Letting the Judge Rest

One of my patients named John, a man who had gone blind because of his diabetes, once commented that being blind wasn't his problem. John's problem was that he couldn't let go of wishing that he were not blind. As soon as his mind began relating to the desire for things to be different, he began to feel angry and frustrated, which made him feel tense and irritable. His frustrated feelings re-engaged stored memories of other times when he had felt helpless and angry. John's wish was to break out of that mind-set and learn to live with his blindness.

John was caught in the most familiar bind of them all—wishing for life to be different. That is the essence of suffering. The only way to derail that suffering is to let go of desires—the wants and fears that prevent us from living in the present. Desiring things we don't have—the "if onlys"—and desiring to avoid the things we don't want—the "what ifs"—are the ego's main preoccupation. Desires are always the cause of suffering—of falling out of the present into the ego's ruminations.

How many times has your mind told you that you could be happy *if* you lost ten pounds? made more money? had your health? Then, even if these things come to pass, you just move on to the next set of conditions for happiness. The conditions are like the proverbial carrot that dangles in front of the donkey. You never reach them.

Happiness can occur only at the moment that desires cease. At that time the mind is still. It's not thinking, not wanting or fearing; it is totally absorbed and attentive. Can you remember the experience of being really thirsty on a hot summer's day and the contentment of taking a drink? Every time the mind is completely absorbed—perfectly mindful—it grows still, and you automatically experience the background of unconditioned consciousness—the Self—that is always there but is usually hidden behind the ripples of the mind. *Because gratification of a desire leads to the temporary stilling of the mind and the experience of the peaceful, joyful Self, it's no wonder that we get hooked on thinking that happiness comes from the satisfaction of desires. This is the meaning of the old adage, "Joy is not in things, it is in us."*

Although getting something we want or avoiding something we don't can give us peace briefly, it never lasts. The mind is like a junkie—on the prowl for its next hit of peacefulness by looking to satisfy a desire. Between satisfactions, the experience is generally unpleasant. True peacefulness comes from abandoning the illusion that satisfying desires brings pleasure. It is called even-mindedness. In that state, you regard every moment as an opportunity to live fully, to be aware. Instead of doing the dishes with the attitude that life is on hold until the unpleasant chore is over, you can choose to do the dishes mindfully, observing the sensations of the water, the bubbles, the feel of the plates. In the state of mindful observation, there are no more judgments about pleasant or unpleasant. The mind grows still, and you can feel the contentment of the Self.

A patient named Sabrina once called me during her first week at the Mind/Body Group. Sabrina's mind had become very still in meditation, and her breath had become so slow that it hardly moved. Time lost its meaning, her body filled with exquisitely pleasurable sensations, and she felt what she could only describe as total joy and peace—unconditional love and a unity with all things. Descriptions of such states are common if you read the lives of the saints or the poetry of the Indian ecstatic poets. The problem Sabrina had, though, was getting trapped in the wheel of desires. On the one hand she feared the "what if" such an experience led into other states that might not be so pleasant—the old fear of losing control. When the experience didn't repeat itself, that fear gave way to "if only" it would happen again. Sabrina judged her other attempts to meditate as worthless. The experience could not happen, of course, as long as she was holding on to making it happen, because the mind could not be still from its judgments.

I gave Sabrina the same advice that a meditation teacher once gave me: "Don't make any appointments and you won't have any disappointments." This means adopting a state of even-mindedness where you are free to "go with the flow," learning from whatever circumstances arise. Alice's attitude toward her recovery from brain damage is a great example of even-mindedness. In taking things as they unfolded, she avoided the inevitable suffering of "if only" and "what if," finding a powerful teacher in what could have been cause for suffering.

Finding peace of mind presents us once again with the challenge to let go. Developing the capacity of taking a breath and backing up into the position of the Witness—the observing Self—is the fastest mode for learning to be mindful. Breathing while noticing that you are experiencing anger is mindfulness. Being so stuck in the experience of anger that you are overcome by it is suffering. The highest ideal of self-understanding comes when a person's ego has retired to the extent that praise and blame are treated equally. There's no puffing up if things go well, and no shriveling away if things go poorly. This is surely a high goal, so it's helpful to remember Einstein's words that "Nobody is able to achieve this completely but the striving for such achievement is in itself a part of the liberation and a foundation for inner security."

❧ Suggestions for the Reader

1. Continue watching your mind. Identify the kinds of desires, the "if onlys" that separate you from being happy now, and the "what ifs" that could deprive you of happiness later.

You may find that your ego revolves around a few repetitive concerns. Write these down. When they occur, congratulate yourself for becoming aware of them. Practice using your breathing as a reminder to let them go. Sometimes it helps to write your anxieties down on a pad so that you can take appropriate action on them at a time that you set aside for that purpose. There's no point worrying about cleaning the house or writing a report or having a conversation before it happens. Do things as a matter of conscious choice, chipping away at unconscious conditioning.

2. Choose at least one activity each day to carry out mindfully—with your full attention, like a meditation. If you are chopping vegetables, chop vegetables. Absorb yourself in the colors, the textures, the motions. If you are drying off after a shower, just dry yourself. It feels great. Richard Alpert, the Harvard psychologist who spent years studying consciousness, sums up mindfulness in the message *Be here now*. Put up a few signs around the house as reminders. The practice is easy; it's remembering to do it that's hard.

3. Don't let your ego bully you and scare you off. Old patterns are hard to change, and usually, as soon as you try, they seem to get stronger in response. This is natural. Many people think they are worse off than before when they start to notice themselves. You are no worse off; you have simply realized what goes on inside. Awareness is the first step to making new choices. It is worth the temporary discomfort to get to know yourself.

4. Use mindfulness to cope with pain and anxiety. I discussed how to do that in the last chapter. Keep trying. If you feel anxious feelings arising inside, try to witness them. Instead of getting stuck in judging, be the observer. By not engaging the mind in battle, by watching and letting go, it will soon become quiet. One very anxious patient, Elizabeth, was

a twenty-eight-old housewife. Her frequent panic attacks were so severe that she thought she was dying. Then one day she said to herself, "Okay, so I'm dying. Do I want to die all full of fear and uptight, or do I want to die peacefully?" She dropped back into her breathing and began to witness the physical sensation of panic. Soon she began to feel peaceful. Needless to say, she didn't die. Since there was no medication that helped Elizabeth with her panic attacks, she believed that mindfulness was her only resource. That motivation was important in helping her apply the lessons when she needed to.

5. *An additional note:* Many people need the help of a seasoned traveler to negotiate the forbidden territories of the mind. Psychotherapists are individuals who have been trained in the mind's maps and have thoroughly explored their own maps. It is often an excellent idea to get safe passage by starting your journey with some therapy.

Audiotapes of mindfulness meditation with Dr. Jon Kabat-Zinn can be ordered from Stress Reduction Tapes, University of Massachusetts Medical Center, Worcester, Massachusetts 01605.

5

Mind Traps: Outwitting the Dirty Tricks Department of the Mind

Two monks were walking by a river at daybreak in the early spring. Swollen with melted snow, the river coursed above its banks, immersing the local footbridge, the only crossing for miles in either direction, under two feet of water. A young woman in a silk dress stood by the riverbank, terrified of the rushing water. Seeing the monks she flashed them a look of pleading. Without a word, the first monk scooped her up in his arms, held her aloft as he struggled across the submerged bridge, and set her down on the far bank. The two monks then continued walking in silence until sunset, when the vows of their order allowed them to speak.

"How could you have picked up that woman?" sputtered the second monk, his eyes blazing with anger. "You know very well that we are prohibited from even thinking about women, let alone touching them. You sullied your honor. You are a disgrace to the whole order." He shook his fist at his companion.

"Venerable brother," said the first monk, "I put that woman down on the other side of the river at sunrise. It is you who have been carrying her around all day."

My patients always laugh at this old Zen teaching story, because it's so typical of the way the mind holds on to a situation, creating suffering long after the incident has passed. It's much harder to be the first monk, putting down the burden by the edge of the river so that it doesn't become a problem that's carried through the day or even for life. While it's easy to see that letting go is much more comfortable than holding on, how can letting go be learned?

Learning to Let Go

In Southeast Asia hunters use a clever trap for catching monkeys. The hunter hollows out a huge pumpkin-like gourd, taking care to leave the shell intact except for a hole just large enough for him to push a banana inside. By and by a monkey will happen along, discover the banana, and stick his hand in the gourd to get it. As soon as the monkey clutches his hand around the banana, he's trapped—hand and banana will not fit through the hole. The poor monkey seals his own fate because his mind cannot give up the idea of grabbing the fruit. He can't let go. The monkey is quite literally a prisoner of his own mind.

Human beings, unlike monkeys, have *awareness* and *choice* at their disposal, the two keys to escape from any bind. The monkey's first obstacle is that he doesn't recognize that holding on to the banana is the source of his problem. Without some awareness of what has happened, he can't choose to let go. Like our primate brethren, we frequently fail to recognize that within our minds is the power to let go and create a different situation. Instead we find it easier to place the blame on the pumpkin or any other immediate circumstance we associate with our suffering.

Some months ago I was standing at the stove preparing string beans, the last step before dinner, when my seventeen-year-old son, Justin, entered the kitchen. He is a wrestler, and when he stands at the open refrigerator, I sometimes feel as though he could inhale the food right off the shelves.

"Dinner's almost ready," I said, but he took out an apple anyway.

He leaned against the counter, eating his apple while I frantically raced to snap the tips off the string beans before the water boiled. "You know, Mom, I'll bet Aunt Sandy spends a hundred dollars a week on cabs. Why doesn't she buy her own car like the rest of the world?"

"It's not that easy," I said. I moved around him to the sink and scooped the rest of the raw beans out of the colander. "She lives in the city and she'd have to rent a parking space. That's expensive. Plus, there are loan payments, insurance, and gas, not to mention general maintenance and repairs—it could cost her as much as taking cabs. Besides, she *likes* taxis."

"But she could get a great car for six grand—that's only about ninety bucks a month." He picked up a string bean, snapped it in two, and began tossing the halves from one palm to the other.

"Well, Justin, maybe Aunt Sandy wouldn't settle for an economy car." The water was just starting to bubble. I picked up the beans in both hands. "Even a moderately priced sedan or sports car can cost twelve to fifteen thousand." The beans hit the water with a soft splash.

He snorted. "What a waste!"

"It's not a waste," I said. "Which costs more—a cheap car that falls apart in three or four years or an expensive car that lasts ten?"

He made a sour face. "You don't have to spend a fortune to get a good car." He dropped the two halves of the string bean on the counter.

When the pot came back to a rolling boil, I waited thirty seconds, then turned down the gas. I could feel Justin watching me, wondering how far he could push his dear old mother.

The handle of the pot was still hot and I grabbed it without thinking. I yelped. My fingers flew off the handle. In a second I had pushed past Justin and was running cold water over my singed fingertips. "It's not that important! What makes you such an expert on cars, anyway? Why don't you make yourself useful for a change instead of worrying about how everybody else is spending their money?"

Justin stared at me. There are times when I look at my son and I see my own startled reflection. I laughed. Why were we so concerned about a hypothetical car that no one was even planning to buy?

Justin pulled the pot off the burner and nudged me away from the sink. "Look out or you'll really get burned."

I listened to what was really going on in my mind, the real subject of the conversation. It wasn't cars, of course. Both my son and I clung tenaciously to hidden agendas. The real conversation was a battle of who-knows-best. Both of us were stuck with our hands in the pumpkin, neither willing to admit that the other could have a valid point of view.

Most parents with adolescent children know this game all too well. The conversation in my own mind was about being in control, about not being wrong. Only by taking a breath and dropping into the position of observer, the witness, as we discussed in the previous chapter, could I have the awareness that afforded me some choice. There was no one to blame and nothing to argue about.

"It's pretty ridiculous for us to be standing here making up Aunt Sandy's automobile," I said.

Justin sheepishly shook the beans in the colander, emptied them into a bowl, and said he'd go call his father for dinner. Only when I pointed out the humor of the debate could we both let go of it and move on to other things. "She'd probably want a Porsche," he said, smiling, as he left the kitchen.

Listening to what was really going on in my mind—the conversation behind the conversation—I recognized my favorite mind trap: needing to be right. Whenever I become aware of it, I remember a brief reminder from psychiatrist Gerald Jampolsky: "Would I rather be happy or would I rather be right?" Yet it's usually hard to relinquish deeply held patterns of behavior. I've often been trapped in my own desire to be right, caught up in the belief that if only others would acknowledge *my* position, then I could let go. I postpone my own happiness. Sound familiar?

Anger, anxiety, and sadness, alone or in combination, are usually the fruits of clinging to a viewpoint. Negative emotions arise from past associations that repeat themselves in our minds and from the response of others who become annoyed with our inflexibility. This chapter explores the part of the mind that makes it hard to let go. Ideally, by understanding the "dirty tricks department" of the mind, you'll gain an insight into how your mind really works. Awareness is the first step to a healthier life. It is a mental stretching that limbers up your perceptions, making you loose enough to let go and thus allowing an element of creative choice to enter your experience.

The Dirty Tricks Department of the Mind

In Chapter 4, we discussed the four parts of the mind. You probably remember the ego, which I characterized as a merciless judge who forever divides the world into good and bad, vigilantly sizing things up to make sure that we get what we want and avoid what we don't want. In so doing, there's a trade-off. We won't be happy, the ego says, unless we get what we want, but the ego sees the world in terms of scarcity, danger, and loss. It taints even those moments of satisfaction with fear—that some unforeseen danger may come along and ruin our happiness. This is how most people think. Like Esau, we sell our birthright for a bowl of porridge. The porridge is the trap: "I can be happy if I get what I want and avoid what I don't want." Our birthright is the inner Witness—the unconditioned awareness that is already fulfilled and happy, *regardless* of outer circumstances.

All of the mind's machinations spring from this single mistake. Our ego churns out an endless stream of mental movies, glittering images of our likes and dislikes, and the more we grasp or flail at these images, the more estranged we become from our Witness, our only real repository of peace.

As we saw in Chapter 4, most of the old baggage that gets transferred onto immediate experience contains stored memories of the ego's basic desires: getting what we want and avoiding what we don't want. The ego, confusing happiness with the fulfillment of these desires, perpetuates our suffering by creating a series of mind traps based on fear. Ignorance, the ego's dynamic, is our primary obstacle to freedom, our greatest hindrance to letting go.

Getting What You Want

Wanting things is a natural part of life. Setting goals and working toward them fuel creativity and invention. The desire to change things activates progress. Wanting, per se, isn't the root difficulty; it's the pernicious attitude that we can't possibly be happy unless we satisfy a certain desire. I once had a patient who had recently divorced. He was so convinced that his happiness depended on being in love that he was miserable without a relationship. His misery, of course, manifested itself as a host of uninvited problems. He became an insomniac, which left him irritable and tense. Tired, he stopped playing racquetball and tennis and became even more tense. Desperate, he tried eating and drinking the problem away, in the process loathing himself more and more. In due course, he developed ulcers and severe headaches. Ironically, by identifying happiness exclusively with a relationship, and not as something within himself, he undermined his chances of attracting a suitable mate.

We suffer to the degree that we make our desires central to our happiness. As my son Justin's sixteenth birthday approached, he began to think he needed a car. Suddenly there was no other way to get to school, to see his friends, even to exist. He poured every spare moment into fulfilling this desire. His first purchase, a forty-dollar heap, held together for two weeks. The very night of its collapse into scrap metal, he set out to get another one. This car lasted four days, until its collision with a school bus on a snowy road. In the following month, while waiting for the insurance settlement, Justin slowly realized that life could go on. A car was not the final referee of his happiness.

Many situations, unfortunately, are not so clear. In marriage, for example, hanging on to the idea that we can't be happy until our spouse behaves like Prince or Princess

Charming blocks our ability to appreciate his or her good qualities. We stay stuck in longing for what we can't have.

Deferring happiness until any condition is met—a new job, a new relationship, a new possession—leads to suffering. In clinging to our desires, we send ourselves a strong statement that things are not okay right now. As life goes on, the feeling of dissatisfaction keeps us hooked to our wants, preventing us from letting go and enjoying the present moment.

Remember your first apartment? Bliss! A place of your own at last. But soon you begin to notice the flaws. The rooms are *so* small. There's never enough hot water. The upstairs neighbors practice their samba steps at 2 A.M. Before long you want to move. You get a bigger apartment. Home free, finally. Until the couple next door has a baby, and the cycle starts all over again. There's never an end to wanting. Whenever a desire masquerades as the thing that separates you from happiness, the rest of life drops into the background. Your desire has become a prison locking you out of life.

Getting What You Don't Want

The other kind of desire we discussed in Chapter 4 is the wish to avoid getting something we don't want. Mentally, each of us creates a cauldron seething with life's potentially painful experiences, and since each of us is unique, the imaginary disasters that bubble to the surface differ with each of us. For one person, the ultimate terror may be a lonely widowhood; another's demon is the thought of losing a job. At an extreme, such worries can totally paralyze their victims.

Recently, my mother was reminiscing about the kidnapping of the Lindbergh baby nearly fifty years ago. My grandfather apparently lost sleep for weeks, fretting about the possible abduction of my older brother, his first grandchild. Eventually he installed locks on every window in my parents' house. Most of the time, the ego's bullying projections never materialize, but that doesn't stop our apprehension. The great sage who writes teabag aphorisms got it right: "Worry is the interest paid on a debt before it comes due."

Mind Traps: Double Jeopardy

The ego tries to stop our suffering by explaining why we hurt. Dividing the world into good and bad, the ego naturally connects painful events with something bad, and the first place it looks is the storehouse of negative opinions we've spent a lifetime gathering about ourselves and the world. Instead of exploring the situation at hand, the ego grabs the solution it knows best—unfounded opinion. The ego hammers these negative beliefs into *mind traps,* mental grillwork that cuts us off from an accurate view of life. Without clarity we have no awareness, and without awareness we have no choices. We end up suffering instead of finding liberation.

Anguish is only part of the price we pay for letting our thinking lapse into mind traps. Certain traps, particularly the ones connected with negative personal beliefs, disillusion, and despair, increase our physical vulnerability to disease.

You may remember the damaging effects of helplessness described in Chapter 1. Martin Seligman, a research psychologist at the University of Pennsylvania, has performed many experiments that demonstrate how most human beings, when consistently placed in situations over which they feel they have no control, are permeated by a sense of helplessness that often extends beyond any specific event. They begin to believe they have no power to change their world. Seligman and collaborators found that if they deprived people of the ability to reduce the noise level in a lab, about two-thirds of them later failed to adjust an irritatingly bright light, although they had the power to do so. They believed themselves helpless.

Seligman paid very careful attention to his subjects' thoughts about unpleasant experiences, and he found his group divided into optimists and pessimists. Those who were pessimists became helpless. Pessimistic thinking about unwanted experiences contains three key ingredients (which, we shall see, also characterize mind traps). Pessimists tend to blame themselves for adverse occurrences; they often characterize such circumstances as lasting indefinitely; and they often conclude that their poor or unpleasant performance in one situation or event will lead to future failure.

A pessimist, should his car skid into a school bus on a snowy day, might think about the event in this way: "I'm such a poor driver. I'll never learn to drive safely. Every time I try something new, I screw it up."

The optimist, on the other hand, might blame the snowy roads, maybe the other driver, or poor visibility. While he might be inclined to take responsibility, he wouldn't take the blame. Nor would he take the accident as an indication he'd never learn to drive safely. ("I'm just a beginner, and beginners have to expect a banged fender once in a while. I'll have to be extra careful until I'm a little more practiced.") Last of all, the optimist wouldn't read the accident as a signpost to the rest of his experience.

Buddhist and Hindu philosophical systems offer amazingly well-developed tools for observing the mind and escaping the mental activities that cause suffering. The *Yogasutras* of Patanjali, an ancient guide to spiritual practice, states in its opening sentence that "yoga is the stilling of the modifications of the mind." These modifications, of course, are the constant, inner chatter and repetitive negative statements that sap so much of our energy. The point of meditation, as originally taught in spiritual traditions, was to achieve awareness of the mind so that thinking could be a matter of choice rather than of habit.

The art of stilling the mind, like all arts, takes time and practice. The information on mind traps is enough to get started, a very rudimentary map of a complicated territory. Reread the instructions in Chapter 2 on meditation. Remember to be the observer. Meditation is a microcosm of how to use your knowledge of mind traps. In meditation you remember for a few seconds to follow your breathing, repeat the mantra, and identify with the Inner Self or Witness rather than with the mind. Then a sticky thought floats by and catches your attention. Off you go on a wild goose chase of associations until you finally remember to be aware ("Oh! There I go—thinking again") letting go and returning to the breath. Discerning mind traps is similar. Usually we completely identify with the mind's contents. Then we remember to step back and observe, asking ourselves if our thoughts resemble any of the mind traps. Inevitably, the emotion of the moment will sweep us away again. Still, constant effort to observe, to remember the Witness, will bear fruit.

Attuning yourself to the devious ways the ego works gives you the power to listen to yourself in a new way, to unmask the hidden staging behind the drama of events. Recognizing the pattern of a mind trap in your response to a particular experience won't bring instant release. Mind traps are strong precisely because we've been practicing them for years, and undoing them takes concentration and an almost heroic effort. Awareness is the price of happiness, no matter how painful. Only when you can identify where your ego traps you can you let go and begin to make choices based on facts.

Let's begin our discussion of mind traps with a commonplace occurrence, a domestic squabble that ruins the day. Listen carefully to Judy's thoughts and try to sort them into *opinion* (unfounded belief concocted in her mind) and *fact*. Opinions, rather than events or situations, cause our suffering.

It's Friday, 7:30 A.M. Both Judy and John are rushing to leave for work. It's Judy's turn to make breakfast this morning and she's gotten off on the wrong foot by oversleeping fifteen minutes. She tosses two bagels into the toaster and heads for the bathroom. A few minutes later the aroma of incinerating bagels interrupts her application of eyeliner. She rushes out to the kitchen. "It's too late," John says, holding the smoking bagels under the faucet. "So much for breakfast."

Judy gives him a poisonous glare. "We wouldn't be out of bagels if *somebody* had done the shopping."

"We wouldn't need more bagels if you'd gotten the toaster fixed on Tuesday, like you said you would. Besides, *somebody* was working on your car during all his free time, if you remember correctly."

Judy snaps that her car is running worse than ever. John tells her to fix it herself next time. They storm out of the house, and both of them nurse a grudge for the rest of the day.

Let's follow Judy's thoughts as her ego trundles out the heavy guns, the six most common mind traps. Bear in mind that although we're examining the traps in order, the mind is never as tidy; thinking jumps from one trap to another, according to our idiosyncrasies.

Trap 1: Negative Personal Beliefs

Judy: "I'm *so* scatterbrained. I never get organized to get out of here on time. Things are always falling apart around me. I suppose I shouldn't expect things to be different. I'm a lousy cook anyway."

The heart of this trap is a mean, self-deprecating opinion of oneself without the evidence to back it up. Judy, in fact, is a vice president of a large Boston bank. She obviously didn't climb the corporate ladder by behaving like an scatterbrain. She makes her bad situation worse by telling herself that she'll never get out of this bind. Like one of Seligman's helpless subjects, she assumes that the situation will last forever and that it reflects the tenor of her entire life. Yet everything about Judy's kitchen—pots hanging overhead within easy reach and professional utensils lined upright in a magnetic rack by the counter—epitomizes neatness and organization. Contrary to her internal statement, things in her life never "fall apart." Judy's mind has cooked up "scatterbrained," a negative personal belief that doesn't even remotely correspond to how most people would characterize her.

When you can't explain away your problems, it's easy to assume you're inadequate, easy to dredge up some fabricated weakness. Snapping at a child and then concluding, "Well, I guess I'm just a rotten parent," doesn't bring any awareness into the situation. Such statements never ask *why* you behaved as you did or *how* you behaved. Instead, they revolve around badness, around your not being good enough. They just assume you're at fault, not all the same as *taking responsibility for understanding the situation*. Trap 1 completely dismisses your personal power· and freedom of choice.

People who fall into this first mind trap often lacerate their self-esteem with distorted images of their bodies. Steve

Maurer, the Associate Director of the Mind/Body Program, tells the story of a friend who was commonly regarded as the most beautiful woman in his social circle. She had a truly distinguished nose, similar to Sophia Loren's. One day she appeared in bandages, announcing that she'd gotten her nose straightened. All her life she'd thought her nose was ugly, an opinion that literally flew in the face of reality.

At an extreme, viewing the body in such negative terms can lead to bulimia, to anorexia, or even to death. Although eating disorders are usually associated with females, they're often present, though hidden, in men as well. Witness the emaciated male runner. A growing health consciousness unfortunately encourages unrealistic expectations of our bodies. New diets, video workouts, and health clubs spring up every day, each touting our potential for the perfect shape. A colleague of mine returned from a two-week vacation looking rather drawn and thin. Concerned, I commented on her loss of weight. To my surprise, she interpreted this as a compliment. "Thanks, Joan. After all, in our society you can never be too rich or too thin."

Not everyone manifests this trap in such dramatic physical terms. Yet the thoughts of its victims steam down the rails of the same track—a conviction first of all that you're bad and, secondly, that you'll never be good enough (good enough for *what* is a question with a thousand individual answers). Under an assault from Trap 1, your self-esteem can erode into nothing.

Trap 2: Social Beliefs

Judy: "John shouldn't have snapped at me like that. Burning the bagels made me want to crawl back into bed and start the day over. He should have given me some support and love. Husbands and wives are supposed to support each other. I thought that's what marriage was all about. Come to think of it, our marriage isn't what it should be."

Should is a code word with the force of society behind it. All of us hold beliefs about how life should proceed. Everyone benefits if we agree to stop at red lights, honor the Ten Commandments, and forbid the use of guns to settle arguments. In everyday parlance, however, we use *should* to express displeasure at not getting what we want. Judy tells herself she wouldn't be suffering over the bagels if she had a more supportive husband. It's quite possible for someone to burn the breakfast bagels and still be happy, but Judy has cut herself off from this possibility. *I won't be happy*, she tells herself, *unless life meets these conditions*.

Hurling an angry broadside of *shoulds* at another person only provokes more suffering. *Should* implies that you're perfect and the other person is to blame. We can hardly blame John if his first response is to defend himself, and most likely he'll fire off an irate counterattack. *Unless John behaves as he should, then it's his fault I'm unhappy* (or so Judy believes).

In a variation of Trap 2, Judy could have turned her wrath against herself: *I should have known better than to try toasting the bagels and applying my makeup at the same time*. Shoulds serve only to plunge us deeper into our bad feelings about ourselves, feelings that easily boil over into anger—as they did for John and Judy on the morning of the bagel fiasco.

Trap 3: Doing It My Way

Judy: "So ask yourself, who does the lion's share of the work around here? John hasn't the slightest idea about all I do to make this place run smoothly. He thinks he's Mr. Sensitive if he offers to toast the bagels alternate mornings. Big deal. The creep can toast his own lousy bagels from now on."

Of all the traps we've examined thus far, number 3 has the most zing to it. The defeatist, helpless attitude of the first trap gave way in Trap 2, as Judy's mental conversation shifted position to a little bit of anger. In Trap 3 Judy inflates her anger and blame and throws it at John, thereby asserting her independence from the situation.

For most of us, this kind of thinking inevitably leads to separation from others. In the grip of Trap 3, you're absolutely convinced of the rightness of your position, and nothing can make you change your mind. Being right becomes more important than anything else. Adolescent children often have this perspective, which is a natural part of growing up. An adolescent forges his own identity by separating from his parents, sometimes rebelliously. "It's my ear and I'll wear a safety pin through it if I want to!"

In an adult, such insistence on being right traps one into a turtle's-eye view of the world and reduces the realm of choice to a slit of daylight glimpsed between halves of a shell. Safe, but with limited options. When Justin and I discussed his aunt's buying a car, we could have terminated the conversation in Trap 3 language, each of us withdrawing behind our opposing convictions of rightness. Communication would have stopped. Awareness would have stopped. Choice would have stopped. Marriages turn arid and die when husband and wife make a habit of having too many conversations in this trap. Relying on anger and blame to create a sense of independence does more than just cut off relationships; it can lead to the quirky antisocial behavior that expresses contempt for society's rules or, if carried one step further, contempt for society's laws, or criminality.

In the case of Justin and me, we were able to let go because I identified the trap, took responsibility for my behavior, and used the interaction as a way to stimulate awareness in both of us. Neither one of us had to be wrong.

Trap 4: Rationalizing

Judy: "John must be really tired this morning. That's why he snapped at me. I'll bet he was tossing and turning all night because of that tennis elbow. That must be it. I know that if I don't sleep well, I blow things way out of proportion. He'll probably apologize tonight."

Rationalization, Trap 4, is the process of assembling an explanation of events that satisfies us intellectually because it seems to conform to our perceptions. In fact, we often invent feelings or even whole identities for other people. What a surprise when they behave like themselves instead of our fantasies about them. Judy has no reliable indication that John lost any sleep or was bothered in the slightest by his tennis elbow. Nevertheless, they did have an unpleasant exchange this morning and Judy needs to find a plausible explanation why.

Like all traps, rationalization has no foundation in actual experience. The bits and pieces of information that go into its construction are frequently projections of our own thinking. We attribute to others our own modes of feeling and acting. Since no two people think exactly alike, this strategy fails. We can always intuit when we're rationalizing. If Judy believed her explanation, she could let go of the dogfight over the bagels. But because she instinctively recognizes that John's tennis elbow isn't the real issue, she still feels terrible. Whenever you devise a solution that *sounds* like common sense, but your head and your heart can't come together on it, you're in Trap 4.

Trap 5: Disillusionment

Judy hurries home early from the bank, then remembers that John will be at an office meeting until seven-thirty. She mixes herself a martini, collapses into an armchair with her drink, and reaches for the pack of cigarettes she bought on the way home. She quit smoking three years ago, but there's nothing like a smoke and a drink when you've got the blues.

Judy: "I might as well face it. Things will never change between us. If we can't get along after seven years of marriage, how can we even think about having children? Maybe I'm just not cut out for marriage. Maybe I ought to get a divorce."

Disillusionment sets in when the other traps just aren't up to the job. We tried, right? We did our best, and it just wasn't good enough. If the other traps don't satisfy us, we seek some temporary escape—a drink, a cigarette, a cup of coffee—something to keep the failure at bay.

Judy sips on her martini, raking back through her marriage, her encounters with other men, stitching together a picture of incompetence to validate her sense of having blown it with John. Notice how she piggybacks her disillusionment onto the powerless, negative self-beliefs of Trap 1: "I'm just not cut out for marriage" (in other words, she's no good at it).

Wallowing in self-pity and self-blame, Judy *thinks* she knows why she's stuck in her present situation—she's not good enough, or John's not good enough, or any of the other reasons we've explored in previous traps—but her reasoning has no basis in reality. Thinking she knows the answer when she doesn't places her in a very dangerous position because it shuts the door on questioning that might reveal other, more realistic possibilities.

Trap 6: Despair

Judy: "John's abusing me—it's the story of my entire miserable life. Just give me a good situation and I guarantee to mess it up. They'll probably fire me for screwing up that big account at the bank today. My back hurts and I've got a pounding headache. About the only thing that would help now is another drink."

Alcoholism, drug addiction, and a host of other self-destructive behaviors, including suicide, are common answers to despair. Paradoxically, intense misery may be just the motivation we need to re-examine things. Mythologies of every culture contain the tale of a hero who triumphs only in the face of extreme defeat or a close encounter with death. In Western culture we have the phoenix that rises from its own ashes and the myth of Oedipus. The Oedipus tale is usually presented in its truncated form, ending with the hero's self-inflicted blindness. In other versions Oedipus's suffering teaches him compassion, allowing him first to regain his throne and then elevating him into the pantheon of the gods. In the longer version Oedipus is an archetype of crucifixion and resurrection, not the guilt-ridden servant of unpredictable fate. The Chinese word for *crisis* combines the characters for *danger* and *opportunity*. No society exists without this pattern deeply embedded in its consciousness.

Judy has not yet reached this point of extreme self-disillusionment. Perhaps instead of a drink, she settles for a nap. She can't sleep her problem away, but a little bit of peace from her destructive chain of thought is probably her best temporary solution. Naps, like meditation, allow you to let go of obsessive thoughts. She wakes up feeling refreshed; some perspective has returned. In the next part of the chapter we'll take a look at some of the ways she can expand her awareness and avoid falling into mind traps.

The Three Levels of Understanding

Level 1: The Beginner's Mind

Judy: "Whew, what a crazy day. I don't know how these tiffs get started or why I get so bent out of shape. You'd think I'd have more answers, but I guess I don't. All I know is that we fight more and more. I really don't understand why. What's this all about anyway?"

Understanding begins with an admission of our ignorance. A Zen story about a college professor speaks directly to this point. The professor becomes curious about the reputation of an old monk, revered for his wisdom, and decides to pay him a visit. The monk welcomes the professor to the temple, invites him inside, and installs him on a comfortable cushion.

"Do you like tea?" the monk asks, passing the professor a cup. The professor nods, holding the cup as the monk pours a thin stream of tea from a heavy iron kettle. The liquid quickly rises to within an inch of the brim and the professor glances upward. The monk continues to pour. The tea rises to the brim and flows over the edge, but the monk keeps pouring.

The professor leaps to his feet, dropping the cup. "What are you doing?"

The monk pauses, picks up the cup, fills it, and then offers it to the professor. "This teacup is like your mind. You can't hear anything new because it's already full."

As long as we're convinced that we know the cause of our suffering, evidence to the contrary, we're like the professor. Without letting go of old explanations, we can't open ourselves to other possibilities. Judy takes her first step toward understanding when she acknowledges the futility of her so-called solutions. After a disagreeable exchange, sincerely admitting that you don't know how it came about helps to cut off the canned explanations, the negative opinions and blame, and makes you more receptive to unexplored possibilities.

Suzuki Roshi, the great Zen master, summed it up: "In the beginner's mind there are endless possibilities; in the expert's there are few." He exhorted his students to cherish the suppleness they brought to meditation as beginners, the openness that you can have only when you acknowledge that you don't know what you're doing. If you want to stop suffering, you have to approach your problem with an empty teacup, with the mind of a beginner.

Level 2: Taking Responsibility

Judy: "I wonder if something in *my* behavior made John snap at me. Lately I've noticed that the times he gets angry are when I'm already feeling bad."

Without resorting to blame, Judy accepts that her own behavior may be contributing to her marital difficulties. She notices a pattern—a connection between John's anger and her own self-doubts. A breakthrough like this becomes possible only after you jettison all of your previously cherished opinions. An obvious pattern reveals itself only when you're clear enough to see it. Accepting responsibility for your behavior is the opposite of blaming yourself; it implies a faith in your ability to change, to transcend the negative thinking of mind traps.

Also, by thinking in terms of her behavior, instead of blame, Judy automatically lowers the emotional stakes of the encounter. She can discuss her observations with John and enlist his aid in probing her recent insight. They're still a long way from understanding, but they're becoming aware, trying to shift their roles from victims to observers. She and John decide that if they can't maintain their new perspective—trying to be more aware of their thinking and communicating about it openly—they'll try couples therapy. Perhaps their most important insight extends far beyond their present difficulties; that is, they don't have to follow the same mindless pattern in their relationship; they can change.

Level 3: Wisdom

Understanding is progressive. We have to work at it. No one can undo the habits of a lifetime without wrestling with those habits again and again and again. I've presented a model of understanding in three levels to give you a sense of direction and because each stage of understanding builds on its predecessor. Unraveling any negative encounter, with ourselves or others first requires a sense of perspective. That's why, psychologically speaking, you're asked to clear the decks of your opinions in Level 1. The next stage prepares you for new insight. Taking responsibility for your actions is another way of expressing your commitment to change. Level 3, then, represents the insight that arises from a calm, blame-free perspective. Every situation, naturally, has its own teaching. Wisdom, unlike rationalization, always feels like relief. Once you understand that your goal is to change rather than accuse, your mind will come to your aid.

Judy, taking the steps outlined in the first two levels, analyzes her situation from a new perspective, refusing to let her previous history contaminate her observations. Notice the difference between her present thinking and her previous interpretations based on mind traps. At last she has a chance of resolving her problems.

"I notice John gets angry when I start blaming him for my problems. I got up late and I knew there was no way I'd have time to get dressed, make breakfast, and still reach the train on time. I wanted John to help out with breakfast—without my having to ask him. When that didn't happen, I cranked up my old song and dance about feeling unsupported, about how nobody loves me. Burning the bagels made it worse. Then I started to hassle him about hurrying up, throwing in a few comments about how much work I have to do in the morning, just to make him feel guilty. What a mess! No wonder he snapped at me. Of course he's going to blow his top if I make him feel bad about himself! I guess I've gotten into the habit of doing that to him. I've got to learn how to ask for help—not beat around the bush. I can't expect John to be a mindreader."

🎎 Suggestions for the Reader

C A U T I O N ! ! !

The most common disaster in applying this system is in thinking that you have someone else's number. *Don't analyze other people's traps.* To do so practically guarantees you of falling into Trap 3 and creating a lot of anger. Generally, attempts to analyze other people fail because we don't have enough data. It's easy to get stuck in opinions and projections—thinking that the other person's mental processes are the same as our own. Typically, they're not. *You can only be responsible for your own process.*

Choose three specific incidents like Judy's over the next week. Write down the thoughts you have about the incidents and reflect on them. Identify your traps. Remember, you may fall into any trap, in any order. Don't try to order your thoughts by traps. Just number the thoughts as they come back to you, taking care to distinguish between the literal conversation you're having with yourself and your hidden agenda, the root cause of your suffering. Although it may seem painful at first, the real pain is in remaining unaware. Only awareness can open you to the range of choice necessary for freedom.

As you apply the exercise to your thoughts throughout the day, you may find your mind returning again and again to certain favorite traps. I mentioned that one of my own favorites is Trap 3, doing it my way. Needing to be right gets me into a lot of trouble. At this point a few positive statements can be useful in helping you to let go. When I become aware I've let myself fall into Trap 3, I always ask myself, "Would I rather be right or would I rather be happy?" The question keeps my awareness focused and lessens the conditioned pull of my mind. I've provided a list of various such questions and statements you might use against each of the traps, but you ought to develop your own affirmations. They're antidotes to mindless thinking patterns, and the more meaning you invest in such an affirmation, the greater its power to restore you to equilibrium.

- I don't know. (Use this when you find yourself circling between traps without any resolution.)
- Would I rather be right, or would I rather be happy?
- Is it really worthwhile to think-feel-act this way?
- How can I make this situation creative?
- Let go of that banana!
- I could choose peace instead of this. (Also from Jampolsky.)
- Thy will, not mine, be done.
- How would *X* (Jesus, Buddha, or whichever teacher/role model has meaning for you) approach this problem?

Judy's step toward awareness and understanding is just that—a first step. Neither I nor any other therapist has a magical panacea for suffering. Mind traps, levels of awareness—these are simply one possible structure, out of hundreds of potential choices, to help encourage awareness. Old ways of thinking exert incredible force. Human beings learn by association and repetition and find it difficult to drain the charge out of old beliefs and habitual patterns of reaction that have a lifetime of voltage in them. Old patterns are like riverbeds. You can build a dam, re-educate the flow of the river, and lead it in a new direction, but an unusually heavy rain can easily overwhelm the dam, leaving the river to rush back to its familiar course.

Begin your analysis of mind traps with the small emotional upsets in your life. By practicing with these, you will gradually increase your strength to resist the conditioned pull of larger dilemmas.

6

Reframing and Creative Imagination

It is often the frame of reference through which we view the world that creates the meaning of things. The same set of facts can look very different when viewed through someone else's eyes. When she came to the Mind/Body Clinic, Rhoda was a thirty-two-year-old software engineer who just had changed jobs for the fourth time in three years. According to her, the reason for her frequent changes was always that one or more male supervisors hated women and purposefully made things difficult. The problem, however, was not so much in the men but in the "glasses" through which Rhoda saw the world.

The cause of Rhoda's problem lay in her upbringing. Rhoda's father, who died when she was fourteen, had come from a family of five brothers, where males were revered. As fate would have it, Rhoda's father had three daughters. His disappointment grew with each child. This unfortunate man was totally unaccepting of his daughters. As a child, Rhoda had many times mumbled the wish that he would die. When he did die, she, like most children, held herself responsible for her father's death. Every time she thought of him, she relived her feelings of rage and frustration coupled with guilt. Superimposing this negative frame of reference on all men, Rhoda was unable to relate to men in school and at work.

When Rhoda first came to the clinic, she was unable to admit that her problem was in her own perception. As far as she was concerned, she was a liberated feminist who saw men for what they were. This was not true. In order to get better, she needed to reframe her situation.

An Exercise in Reframing

Find yourself a pencil and paper and take a moment on this brainteaser.

It's called the nine-dot puzzle. Here are the rules:

1. Connect all nine dots using *four, straight, continuous lines*, no curves allowed.

2. Your pencil must stay on the paper. In other words, you can't lift it up and make discontinuous lines.

🏵 Try this for a few minutes before reading further.

If you have not found the solution, you're in good company. Here's a hint: *Don't get boxed in by the dots*. Take a good look at the shape your attempted solutions suggest. A square, right? That's exactly the frame of reference that is preventing you from seeing the solution.

▓ Try again for a few minutes before reading further.

If you have found the solution, congratulations! If you haven't found it, see the next page. Actually, very few people solve this riddle, even after the hint. To solve the problem, you have to go beyond the imaginary limitation of the square.

The solution is possible only when the erroneous frame of reference is identified and surpassed. Similarly, Rhoda made progress only after she identified and took responsibility for her own frame of reference.

Richard Bandler and John Grinder, founders of Neurolinguistic Programming (NLP), a powerful scientific method that helps people reframe meanings, tell the story of a woman who was driving her family crazy by being obsessively neat. She vacuumed the rug constantly and became enormously upset if anyone walked on it. Bandler and Grinder first helped the woman into a relaxed state—that is, elicited the relaxation response—where mental connections would be more flexible and new associations could be made. They then had the woman imagine what her house would be like if there were no one there to mess up the rug. No husband to love, no children to delight her. Just a clean rug. She began to associate a perfect rug with being lonely, and a new frame of reference was born. Once she began to see

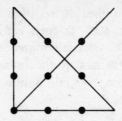

the situation from this vantage point, she delighted in imagining her loved ones returning and walking over her precious rug!

Reframing in Daily Life

All of us have practiced reframing many times, probably without being aware of it. I remember as a high school student babysitting for a six-year-old boy named Mark. As his mother left for the evening, she apologetically told me Mark did poorly with babysitters, often refusing to go to bed. Her advice was that I should let him play in his room until he fell asleep on the floor.

About half an hour after Mark's parents left, I told him to go to sleep. He barely looked up from the puzzle he was playing with and said angrily, "You're stupid and I hate you. I'm not going to bed and you can't make me."

I was stunned by his hostility, but instead of reacting emotionally, I used a tactic my brother Alan had used on me as a child when I refused to go to bed. An insult seemed best. "You look pretty slow," I said. "I'll bet you're the slowest kid in your gym class."

That got Mark's attention, and he looked up. Now he was really mad. "No, I'm not," he yelped.

"Yes, you are." I said calmly.

"No, I'm not," he howled.

"Oh, yeah?" I replied. "Prove it. I'll bet you can't even get into your pajamas before I count to thirty."

He was off like a flash. He came back grinning as I hit twenty-eight.

I was unimpressed. "Not bad, but I'm sure you can't possibly wash your hands and face by the count of sixty." He zoomed out, returning shining clean and triumphant in forty-seven seconds.

I was softening up. "Not bad at all. You're faster than I thought. If you can get your clothes folded and jump into bed by the count of forty, then I will read you a story."

After that, Mark and I were fast friends. My little game was reframing, although I didn't realize it then. I got Mark's undivided attention by meeting him in his cantankerous frame of reference and challenging his athletic prowess. The first step in reframing is acknowledging and understanding the other person's viewpoint—or your own. When I shifted Mark's frame of reference toward going to bed, by capitalizing on his own energy, I allowed him to resist me all the way to bed! Using the energy that is tied up in resistance but channeling it in a new direction, is the mental equivalent of the martial arts, where subtle shifts in balance allow the opponent's energy to be used to your own advantage. In reframing, the opponent is often your own mind-set.

Blocks to Reframing

The first step in reframing is to notice that you are stuck in a frame of reference that is not productive. This is the key. Some forms of being stuck are very subtle, consisting of holding on to opinions that prevent a widened perspective that could be useful. Remember the opinion of our colleague who discounted acupuncture by fitting it into a frame of reference labeled in his own mind as "hypnosis and other crazy stuff"? Other mental sets are more obvious, like Rhoda's problem or the problem with obsessive neatness in Bandler and Grinder's story. Illness itself can be an insidious trap, both because it promotes helplessness and self-pity, which drain away creative power, and also because it can serve as an unconscious way to get important needs met—the secondary gains I mentioned earlier.

The migraine headaches I experienced in my life were a great example of secondary gains. It may be hard to believe that a life of constant pain and unpredictability could have had a hidden benefit that made it worth hanging on to, but this can be part of the story of any continuing illness. My life was an unrelenting struggle to be Miss Perfect. I had to be at the top of my class in school; I needed to feel popular. Without constant recognition of my achievements, I felt quite empty. I was constantly searching for things I could excel in. Of course, there were plenty of things that I had no talent for, but I confined myself to doing the best at whatever I could possibly learn to do. This is a pattern with an obvious up side—it leads to high achievement—and an obvious down side—it leads to stress and agonizing over possible failures. My self-image was entirely dependent on being perfect. What a trap! Clearly I needed an escape. The migraines provided what I needed.

One day, when I was a junior in high school, I came home and locked myself in my room. Everything was happening at once. The French teacher had gone away for a week and left me in charge of his class. The school play in which I had one of the leads was going on to the state drama festival. Since I had won the physics division of the high school science fair, I now had to compete in the state finals. And to top everything, I was fighting with my boyfriend.

My response to this pressure was to blame everyone else. As obvious as my predicament was, I could not see that I had created it. My only way out, where I could have a rest and also let other people know how much they had pressured me, was to have a headache. I had a doozy, which lasted for four days. It's clear that I could not have lived the way I had chosen without a pressure valve—illness—to let off steam. Without it, I would have exploded. Before it was possible to let go of the headaches, I had to realize that I needed time and space for myself and that my sense of self-worth was not dependent on what I could produce. Meditation became the pressure valve that substituted for headaches and also the means to understand how I had become so stuck in a foolish frame of reference.

My own experience helps me to recognize similar behavior in our patients. Several years ago a young man named Bruce joined the Mind/Body Group. At our initial interview he bemoaned his chronic pain problem. It kept him living in his parents' home, working at a job well beneath his capabilities, and prevented him from dating. He told me he was desperate and that he would do anything to relieve his pain. Bruce happened to be one of the lucky people who had a natural facility for meditation. After a few weeks he could concentrate quite well. Soon he learned to breathe with his pain and let go of the spasms that made it worse. He came into the Mind/Body Group on the seventh week looking terrible. When one of the group members asked him if he was in pain, he burst into tears and said: "That's just the problem. For the last two weeks I've had hardly any pain at all. Now I don't know what to do with myself. I'm twenty-seven and I've never moved out of my parents' house. I don't know how to relate to women. I should probably go back to school, but I'm too scared. I don't know how to live any other way. I think I want my pain back."

The group was amazed. Bruce had healed his physical pain, but he now had to face the mental pain, the insecurity, that his physical pain had covered up. It took psychotherapy for Bruce to understand the mental conditioning that underlay his fear, and only through such awareness could he consciously choose to let go of the pain. The hurt and sadness behind the pain stemmed from his abandonment by his father when he was five years old and later his feelings of rejection by his mother when she married a cold, distant man when he was about eight. Bruce's anger was buried so deep that it was literally eating him up from inside.

Bruce's story is important because it illustrates the importance of thinking through how you may benefit from a chronic physical illness. Does it provide attention, security, or an excuse not to move ahead? Is it covering up feelings? These things are powerful unconscious hooks. If you want to let go of your illness, it is crucial to discuss it with your family, because your pattern is enmeshed with theirs. Sometimes other family members have unconscious needs for you to remain sick. Perhaps they derive self-esteem by caring for you or maintain a position of authority because you occupy the position of the needy one. Family therapy is often a tremendous help in identifying unproductive patterns that ensnare family members and may make it impossible to give up the illness.

Keep in mind that as one person within a family system changes, the entire family will change. You may be ready for growth, but the shift in your energy may catch others unaware. If you are prepared for this, you'll find it easier to understand. The process of letting go of a chronic illness will almost always reveal outmoded frames of reference that, because of their familiarity, are hard to relinquish. René Magritte, the wonderful Belgian artist, painted pictures of the human mind. In one, a male figure sits by the beach. In place of his chest there is a bird cage with an open door. One bird sits within the cage. Another perches in the door. Neither will risk letting go of the safety of the cage in order to gain its freedom. Such is the power of old frames of reference. It takes tremendous courage to leave them behind.

The Art of Reframing

Like all techniques, reframing can be used to lead to new understandings or to fool ourselves, enhancing our problems by reinforcing outmoded understandings. I once had a friend who could reframe any situation in which others accused her of being wrong. It was always *their* jealousy or *their* misperception—never hers. She used reframing to stay stuck rather than to grow. At best, reframing challenges the mind, opening the way to let go of old conditioning so that we can wake up to the moment. The following are different ways to use reframing that can lead to growth if the mind is kept open.

Humor

Humor is the natural response to a sudden shift in frames. Remember the old childhood riddle—what is black and white and red all over? The mind searches in the nine-dot square of color. Of course, the solution is not there. The answer, a newspaper, is a member of a totally different set. The sudden shift forces the mind to loosen its grip on "reality" and open to a new understanding. The physiological result is a delightful symphony of good feelings.

My son Justin is an inveterate reframer—the sort who puns and jokes all the time. When he was barely three, we were in my parents' home. The sirens of fire trucks and ambulances disturbed the night air and filled my mother with disastrous imaginings that she shared with everyone else.

Justin quipped, "Gramma, don't worry, it's just Siren and Garfunkel." The resultant laughter completely broke the mood and shifted my mother's frame of reference. I still remember that moment whenever I hear a siren.

Steve Maurer also taught me a joke that I'll never forget. Not only is it a great example of reframing, but the reframe itself is worth remembering. It concerns two great beings, Jesus and Moses, out playing a round of golf. Jesus tees up at a long par-4, 420-yard hole. He sizes up his golf bag and chooses a three iron. Moses shakes his head doubtfully,

"Jesus, it's a long hole. You'll never make it with a three iron; better use a driver."

Jesus smiles and replies, "Arnold Palmer does it." Then he hits the ball with a resounding thwack, and it lands right in the middle of a big water hazard. Moses is feeling forgiving and offers to shag the ball and give his friend another crack at it. So he saunters over to the water hazard and, with great aplomb, parts the waters and picks out the ball. Jesus tees up again, and again he takes the three iron.

Moses laments, "Jesus, you already tried that iron. Believe me, the hole is too long. Here's a driver."

Jesus patiently shakes his head and steps up to the ball. "Arnold Palmer does it," he says. Then he hits it smartly and the ball sails high and short, landing once again in the same hazard. This time he motions Moses to stay put and goes off to shag the ball himself. He approaches the hazard, walks across the water, and picks out the ball. Meanwhile the next foursome has caught up from behind and is looking on, astonished,

"Who does he think he is," says one man. "Jesus Christ?"

"No," says Moses sadly. "Unfortunately, he thinks he's Arnold Palmer."

The reframe to remember is that we are a lot like Jesus in the story. Although our own Inner Self is the source of infinite possibility, creativity, and love, we often identify instead with the limitations of the ego.

Affirmation

In the last chapter I discussed using affirmation to neutralize mind traps. The use of affirmation gradually erodes old ingrained patterns of thinking, substituting a new understanding and a fresh frame of reference. Affirmations can be used not only throughout the day to specifically challenge and counter conditioned thinking, but also at those times of the day when access to the unconscious mind is at its peak. Affirmations help in reprogramming the unconscious. Access to the unconscious is greatest at the edge of sleep and when waking up. You can choose a couple of affirmations to repeat at those times on a daily basis. Just make sure they are framed positively, since the unconscious may not be attuned to *nots*. For instance, "I will not be angry with my spouse" reminds you on some level that you *are* angry. Instead, affirm "I am becoming more loving, understanding, and compassionate to my wife or husband each day." Rather than affirming "I will lose weight," try "I am getting slimmer each day."

Take careful note of your thoughts when you first arise. If you begin the day with negative affirmations—internal moans and groans about all there is to do or the lack of anything, whether time, money, or love—then you have programmed yourself with a mind-set of scarcity. Counteract such thoughts with a positive affirmation of the desired situation. For instance, "I have plenty of energy to do all the things that come my way."

Another time when the conscious mind can easily access the unconscious is during meditation. This works both ways. New understandings can be introduced, but unconscious memories and old patterns can also more easily surface.

Long-forgotten or repressed traumas can suddenly bubble up when the ego's defenses are down and the Judge is temporarily off guard. Many of my patients have commented on this. This situation may be temporarily upsetting, since your mind has invested a lot of energy repressing the traumatic memory. Once out in the light of day, however, such memories are usually less scary than when they were first relegated to the backwaters of the unconscious.

Just as there is the chance that old mental dragons will come out of the closet during meditation, there is the corresponding opportunity to enter new programs into the unconscious. The end of a meditation is the proper time for affirmation. It is also an excellent time for contemplation, when you bring an idea to mind and then just sit with it, noticing what arises. The unconscious is a storehouse of wisdom from past experience that can bring illumination to ideas or problems and help you think of them in an expanded way.

Hypnosis

Most people aren't quite sure what hypnosis is. In reality, it is nothing more than fixating the attention, as in meditation, so that new frames of reference can be established. Dr. Herbert Benson and others have shown that the induction phase of hypnosis, often just a breathing or relaxation technique, produces the physiology of the relaxation response. The second phase of hypnosis, after a receptive mind-set is brought about by the relaxation response, is that of suggestion. Hypnotic suggestion often involves taking a perception and suggesting a new frame of reference that will fit the facts equally well. It is a reinterpretation of reality.

Many examples of hypnosis occur in everyday life. If you establish rapport with someone, so that their attention is completely with you, they are quite open to what you have to say. This is the basis of good communication. It is also the basis of hypnosis.

Persuasive public speakers are good hypnotists. They use gestures and voice inflection to rivet attention. It is known that once attention is fixed, lowered voice inflections are most easily picked up by the unconscious. Like it or not, hypnosis is part of every human interaction. My earlier story of getting little Mark to bed is a wonderful example of what is best called indirect hypnosis, since there was no formal trance induction, just a fixation of attention by my challenge to his speed.

Dreams

Dreams are windows into the unconscious. Since sleep is another time when the Judge is out, what comes into consciousness is uncensored. Many people can recall particularly vivid dreams that occur only once or may be repetitive. Even though they do not consciously understand the dream, they often sense that it is important. Understanding such dreams can be a door to awareness and subsequent reframing. Dreams are often an attempt of the unconscious to produce healing. Consider the following example.

As a child, Janine, now a woman in her thirties, awoke screaming each night for months with the same dream. She remembered it perfectly twenty-five years later. She and her father were standing by a lake. On the other side stood a child of about her age, alone and crying. Her father would give Janine a package and tell her to swim across the lake and give it to the other child. It was well known that a huge snake lived in the water. Janine was afraid to go, but her father was insistent. So each night she would jump in, and halfway across, the snake would come rearing out of the water. Janine would awaken terrified and screaming.

I helped Janine to use the relaxation response to reframe the dream and uncover a new meaning. She centered on her breathing and then began to rerun the dream as if it were happening. In the relaxed state and safe situation, she was able to embark on the dream without coming out of it when she previously had. I asked her to use her imagination to finish the dream. She managed to outswim the snake and deliver the package to the child on the other side. The child was so happy. In the package were delightful foods, special toys, golden coins, and a little blue velvet sack marked "Love." She and the child embraced. Janine felt wonderful. Next, I asked Janine to rerun the dream backward. With some reassurance, she jumped back into the water, again encountering the snake. This time the snake appeared more like a dragon, like Puff from the old Peter, Paul, and Mary song. It scooped Janine up on its back and they frolicked all over the lake. Finally it carried her back to her father. He was so proud of her. He embraced her, stroking her hair and telling her how scared he was to make her swim the lake, but that was what his role was. He had to help her confront her deepest fears so that she could let go of them and be free to rise to her fullest potential.

This one waking dream helped Janine to reframe her relationship with her father. He was a critical person whom she grew up resenting because he was so hard to please. Instead of viewing his criticism and pushiness as devaluing, she began to reflect on how all the pushing had forced her to grow and extend herself. In future interactions with her father, she let go of a lot of the old anger. She no longer responded automatically to his comments by becoming defensive, and for the first time in her life, they developed a close relationship. Janine, of course, was both herself and the child on the opposite shore. Her willingness to confront her fear and swim the distance allowed her to receive the gifts that her father had sent. She was both the recipient and the deliverer. While some people can do this kind of dream work alone, a therapist is usually required. Jungian therapists in particular make significant use of the waking dream.

Creativity

The unconscious mind is a storehouse of wisdom that can be drawn upon for creativity. Dreams and reveries have long been associated with creative breakthroughs.

Creativity requires special conditions. First, you generally need some knowledge about a problem. When the solution fails to arise, you can safely assume that you are stuck in a limited frame of reference. Thus a period of letting go often precedes a breakthrough, a novel recombination of the facts. Most research is a synthesis of problem-solving and creativity. In our office there is a cartoon of two scientists standing in front of a blackboard. One is explaining a long equation to the other. In the middle there is a blank space, and at the far right there is a solution. Pointing to the blank space, one scientist says, "And then a miracle occurs."

How do we get miracles to happen? Whether inspiration is a divine gift, a recombining of the contents of the unconscious in novel form, or both, there are certain techniques that favor its occurrence.

The absolute requirement for creativity is blindfolding the Judge. The first part of the creative process needs to be free of inhibitions. Later on, when ideas are fully formed, there is plenty of time to scrutinize them.

There seem to be instances, however, when information or talents beyond what has been stored in the unconscious of the inventor manifest themselves. Jane Roberts said her book, *The Seth Material,* was typed automatically. She did not feel as if she wrote it. Similarly, *A Course in Miracles,* an inspiring Christian text and workbook, came *through* psychologists William Thetford and Helen Schucman. The state required for this sort of creativity, regardless of its source, is letting go.

The letting go produced by meditation or sleep can be used to enhance creativity. Before falling asleep or near the end of meditation, describe the problem to be solved to yourself in clear and simple terms. A question like why is everybody mean to me is not likely to bring up anything other than your usual ruminations. Be specific. For example, "How can I improve my relationship with _____?" If no answer emerges after several days, review the way you are asking yourself the question. Perhaps the question itself is the frame of reference in which you are stuck.

Creative Imagination

When the famous psychiatrist Milton Erikson became paralyzed from polio as a teenager, there were no rehabilitation services available. For a long time he sat on his front porch, watching the world go by. Instead of pitying himself, he used his paralysis to become an acute observer of the subtleties of posture, voice inflection, and hidden meaning.

One day Erikson's parents went out and left him strapped into a rocking chair. Unfortunately, he was too far from the window. As he sat imagining how he could look out, the chair began to rock slowly. He soon found that the more he thought about getting to the window, the more the rocking increased. Over the course of the afternoon, he refined his imaginings to produce the greatest motion and managed to rock himself over to the window! This experience led him to experiment with the effect of thinking about different motions, until gradually he helped himself to recover from the paralysis. It was his acute powers of observation that later formed the theoretical framework of his extraordinary expertise in medical hypnosis and reframing.

The notion that mental reviews of physical activities actually cause muscle movements is well accepted. Many athletes use such a mental review as part of their training routine. The Soviets, in particular, use creative imagination to give their athletes a competitive edge. The more we imagine any situation, the more deeply etched the mental circuits become. The old meditation literature cautions that the mind takes the shape of whatever it habitually dwells upon.

Harvard psychiatrist Steven Locke often leads his patients through this exercise. First, give a sigh of relief and then breathe your way back from three to one. . . . Next, imagine that you are in your kitchen. . . . Go to the refrigerator and look for a big yellow lemon that is inside. Take it out and feel the weight of it in your hand. . . . Notice the round end where the blossom was, and the flat end where the stem was. Run your fingers over the pitted, waxy surface. . . . Take your fingernail and scrape the skin, noticing the spray, smelling the aroma, and feeling the slippery lemon oil between your fingers. . . . Now put the lemon down on the counter and locate a knife. Cut the lemon in half, and as the juice wells up to the surface, lick it off.

Did you notice any physiological reaction to your imagination? Most people notice that their mouths pucker and that they begin to salivate as if they were actually licking a lemon. The fact is that the body cannot tell the difference between what is actually happening and what you are imagining. When you consider all the negative fantasies that run through the mind each day, it's no wonder that the body stores so much tension. Why not purposely substitute positive fantasies by actively guiding your imagination?

Every time you think about something, you are imagining. The details of the process differ from person to person, but everyone has the ability to imagine. When you are fantasizing, whether positively or negatively, what is your experience? Some people's fantasies are best described as a kind of slowed-down form of thinking. Other people are body centered. Others are visually dominant. Still others relate more to fragrance and taste. There is no right or wrong way to imagine. Since you have done it all your life, there is nothing to learn and nothing to fail at. If you still doubt your own imagination, pretend that you have just hired a window washer who asks for a count of the windows in your house to price the job. Close your eyes and count them. Easy, right?

Since the most prevalent disease is fear and identification with the mind, creative imagination can be used very effectively to dis-identify with the cares of the mind and let go into an experience of pleasure that is absorbing. This, by definition, elicits the relaxation response. It is for this reason that many relaxation tapes begin with a sequence of imagining that you are in a special, comfortable place. You are then instructed to pay attention to the details with each of your senses. In that way you can let go of the thoughts in your mind by focusing on something pleasant. You will have the opportunity to try this at the end of the chapter.

Creative imagination is similar to hypnosis. To "get into" it, you first have to let go. The first step, therefore, is to center on breathing or to meditate for a few minutes. In the second step you are mentally suggesting something that is different from your immediate frame of reference. We know that certain "hypnotically talented" people, about 5 percent of the population, can focus so single-mindedly on a suggestion that they can produce exceptional bodily changes. If you touch such a person with a pencil and suggest that it is a hot iron, a blister will actually rise up at that site. Similarly, if a suggestion of numbness is made, minor surgery can be performed with no other anesthesia. While most of us are not so "suggestible," we can still be affected quite noticeably, as demonstrated by the lemon exercise.

There is an important difference between the use of creative imagination and meditation. While imagination is an outgrowth of meditation, the mind is guided into absorption in a directed fantasy. There is a goal. Meditation is not goal directed; instead, it trains the capacities of self-observation and letting go. While many of our patients enjoy working with various tapes of the imagination, we always encourage them do this as an adjunct to meditation rather than just by itself. In that way they can get the benefits of self-awareness and mind control that meditation preferentially develops. Like meditation, creative imagination can be used in long blocks of time or for just a few minutes. The last few minutes at the end of meditation, when the unconscious is most receptive, is the ideal time to practice creative imagination.

Here are the steps to follow for a simple exercise. Since each of us resonates to different images, you can modify the script below to suit your own situation and preferences. Follow it mentally or record it with or without music. Music that you find enjoyable can stimulate imagination and add considerable richness to the experience.

Take a deep breath and let it go with a sigh of relief. . . . On each of the next few out breaths, let go a little more, letting yourself sink down. . . . In a moment you can count back from ten to one, continuing to let go a little more with each out breath. You can use your imagination to help you let go. With each breath, you might float a little higher in a hot air balloon, imagining the feeling of the gently swaying basket. Or you might enjoy lying on a beach, at the tide line, imagining the waves washing over you gently on the in breath and receding, taking with them any tension or disease, on the out breath. . . . Perhaps some other image comes to mind. . . . So count back from ten to one in the way that suits you best. . . .

Now imagine a beautiful sunlit day in a peaceful place. It may be someplace you know or someplace that comes to mind now. . . . Let your senses fill in the details. What is the earth like under your feet? . . . Imagine how the sun feels, soak up the warm glow, and take it deep inside, letting it energize and balance every cell. . . . How does the breeze feel? . . . What are the colors like? . . . Imagine all the things that make the scene beautiful. Are there sounds? Birds or wind or surf? Enjoy yourself there. . . .

Now find a comfortable spot and settle into it. . . . Imagine your breathing as a stream of warm, loving energy. Direct that loving feeling into your head . . . your neck . . . your shoulders. . . . Breathe that feeling of warmth into your arms and hands. . . . Fill your heart with love and let the feeling suffuse your entire torso. . . . Breathe love into your belly . . . your pelvis. . . . Feel it traveling down your legs . . . right to the bottoms of your feet.

Now imagine yourself looking healthy and peaceful. The sunlight is shining very brightly. As you breathe in, let it enter your body like a sunbeam through the top of your head. With each in breath, allow the light to grow brighter and brighter. The light is peaceful and loving. Let go to that love. . . . Now sit quietly in meditation for a few minutes to allow your unconscious mind to absorb and reflect on your experience and then, whenever you're ready, come back and open your eyes.

⚌ Suggestions for the Reader

1. Continue to practice affirmation. When you awaken in the morning, notice what you are saying to yourself. If it is a negative train of thought, substitute a positive affirmation for it. Throughout the day continue to check into your thinking. Avoid helplessness by taking action on things whenever you can and letting go or reframing when appropriate.

2. Practice looking for reframes. How can you see a situation differently so that it becomes a learning experience rather than an exercise in blame or guilt? A big reframe is to love what you have instead of lamenting over what you don't.

3. Try creative imagination. You might use it for problem-solving, imagining a "wise person" within yourself or asking clear and concise questions of your unconscious before bed or during meditation.

4. Use the script at the end of the chapter for a longer exercise in imagination, and check your local bookstore for tapes on creative imagination that seem interesting to you. Although they vary widely in quality, most will give you some good ideas. Cancer patients may particularly enjoy the audiotapes of Dr. Bernie Siegel. You can write for them at ECAP, Inc.,* 2 Church St. South, New Haven, CT 06519. Videotapes of Dr. Siegel's lectures are also available.

---

*ECAP stands for Exceptional Cancer Patients. The determination of these patients to fight the disease can help them become exceptions to the statistics.

7

Healing the Emotions

Peg is a delightful, warm, outgoing young woman who is married to an adoring husband and has two young sons. Peg came to the Mind/Body Clinic for severe migraine headaches that often lasted for up to four days. When we first met, she described herself as a "super mom" and "super wife." She began to cry as she talked about the previous weekend when her husband's two sisters and their families arrived at her home for a day at the pool with no notice. Although extremely angry, she smiled and acted the perfect hostess. She also took a day's supply of Fiorinal, a prescription drug for migraines. When everyone left, she collapsed into bed but was unable to sleep until 3 A.M.

Peg had no trouble telling me how angry she was, but she could not tell her family. And although she focused her fury on her sisters-in-law, the real source of her anger—her parents—remained hidden to her. She explained to me that once in a while she expressed her emotions, yelling at her husband or children. Whenever that happened, they blamed her for being overemotional and out of control. Peg would then have hurt feelings, new anger, and guilt that she had acted so childishly. With little awareness of what she was feeling and why, Peg was like a time bomb. When the pressure got too intense, she exploded into a rage or experienced a migraine instead. When she tried to find solace from her mother, her problem was passed off as premenstrual syndrome. In Peg's mind everything was either the fault of others' selfishness or her fault for not being perfect. She was caught in three mind traps: negative personal beliefs, "shoulds," and doing it her way. In childhood she had learned the role of perfect daughter—safekeeper of the family feelings. She did what she was told, keeping everyone happy. At thirty-four, she had never learned how to say no. In her own words, Peg was a doormat.

Emotional Mind Traps

Learning to be aware of feelings, how they arise and how to use them creatively so they guide us to happiness, is an essential lifetime skill. To begin, let's look first at three common ways of handling emotions.

Denial

At one extreme are people who completely deny feelings. If you ask how they feel, they say fine and mean it, no matter what is going on in their lives.

You may be more aware of how such people feel than they are themselves. The inability to express emotions has been linked with a number of psychosomatic illnesses, from back pain to migraine headaches. While the conscious mind is unaware of the emotion, the unconscious is painfully aware. Since the tension behind the emotion cannot be dissipated consciously, by talking about it or taking some action, the pent-up energy is somatized—expressed through the body.

Overexpression

In this trap, which is the opposite of denial, people are completely fused with an emotion. Instead of having anger, they *are* anger. This is a dangerous state because they can lose control. The intellect is clouded and more primitive impulses prevail.

Last summer my family and I were out fishing on the ocean. A dozen or so boats were gathered around a school of bluefish. Suddenly an enormous boat came bearing down on us at incredible speed. There was no time to move. Fishing lines were snapped. Our boat was swamped and we were soaked. As we looked disbelievingly after the boat, we saw its name emblazoned on the stern—RAGE.

Repression

The third emotional mind trap lies midway between denial and overexpression. Its game is repressing feelings that you consciously know are present but don't think you have any right to experience. This attitude is double jeopardy. Not only do you feel the pain of emotion, but you add the much bigger pain of resisting the emotion. Peg, for instance, didn't believe that it was okay for her to feel anger, so she held it in. Her attitude led to countless situations that only increased her anger as she let people walk all over her.

A Healthy Attitude Toward Emotions

There are three attitudes toward the emotions that lead to their constructive use.

1. **It's natural and human to experience emotions.** What's a human interest story without pain and anger, love and joy? Emotions are the very stuff of life.

2. **You are entitled to feel however you are feeling, whether or not the emotion is "justified."** Neither you nor anyone else has the right to tell you that you shouldn't feel the way you do. It's only through understanding why we feel as we do that we can progress in self-understanding. When someone takes your remark the wrong way and feels hurt, there's no point in telling that person he or she is wrong. If both parties are willing to accept the feeling and look at what caused it instead, real understanding can emerge.

3. **Negative emotions are a real opportunity to enhance self-understanding.** Only by coming to terms with our reactions to ourselves, to situations, and to others can we discriminate the dirty-tricks department of the ego. Only when the ego and its fear and isolation are set aside can we experience our natural state of peace of mind. The positive emotions—love, joy, confidence, peace—are expressions of the Self. They are always present and have an opportunity for expression when we free them by learning the art of emotional balance.

The Myth of Negative Emotions

Negative emotions are not bad. They are human. Most of the time they are appropriate. When someone you love dies, there is a time of sadness, grief, and mourning. If you don't allow yourself to experience the pain, it will crop up in other ways, and the wound of your loss won't heal. If you get sick, the most natural response is to feel depressed at what you have lost and perhaps angry or frustrated. While you don't have to stay stuck in those feelings, that's where most people start. The natural reaction to hurt is anger. If we don't express it, how can we learn and be taught sensitivity to other people?

Helplessness, you may remember from the first chapter, is associated with illnesses as diverse as ulcers, heart disease, and cancer. Helplessness is an attitude of powerlessness, of victimization. So when a feisty cancer patient shows up in my office distressed or furious over his or her illness or some interaction with a physician, a spouse, or the traffic, and then laments that such distress will lead to a recurrence of the disease, I point out that just the opposite is true. It's hiding feelings, believing that you have no right to experience them, and therefore feeling helpless that leads to a more dangerous emotional state and, at least in some cases, to a worse medical outcome.

The only negative emotions are emotions that you will not allow yourself or someone else to experience. Negative emotions will not harm you if you express them appropriately and then let them go, as I will discuss. Bottling them up is far worse.

Love and laughter are, of course, key attitudes for healing, but they can only be experienced after we let go of the negative patterns that block their expression. You can't paste happiness on top of pain like a bandage and expect good results. It takes patience to work emotions through.

Restoring Balance to the Emotions

Before you can adjust your emotional balance, you have to understand your current emotional style. Do you deny, repress, or overreact? Sometimes we do fine with some emotions, but don't know how to handle others. People's emotional styles can be very different. Each of us comes from a family and from a very different set of life circumstances that have left a unique emotional imprint on us. In some families it's okay to be angry but not sad. In others it's okay to be helpless but not angry. In some families only positive emotions are allowed.

Men, in general, are less accustomed to recognizing their emotional states than are women, since in many families males are rewarded for hiding their feelings—appearing strong and imperturbable. Although there are many cases where this kind of conditioning is reversed, many of my married patients tell a similar story about the difference in male/female emotional styles.

The man complains that his wife is overemotional. The woman complains that her husband is too rational, insensitive to her emotions and his own. She says, "I'm feeling sad; my friend Linda and I had a big fight." Instead of comforting her and validating her right to feel sad, her husband prepares the intellectual equivalent of a legal brief, listing the reasons why she should think differently and trying to figure out who's to blame. She ends up thinking her husband doesn't care about her because he flew right past her emotional needs. He ends up thinking that she's hysterical and unreasonable when his attempts to solve her problem rationally end up making her feel worse.

Any intimate relationship requires an awareness of our own emotional style and that of the other person. It doesn't mean that both people have to have the same style, only that they have to respect the other person's style. If the husband in the above example is aware that his wife experiences her emotions strongly and that it's okay for her to be that way, he can avoid the fight. If he starts the interaction by reflecting back her sense of upset and saying something like "Gee, honey, it looks like you really feel bad about this fight" and then gives her a hug, she will feel supported and understood.

At that point she might benefit from his rational perspective. She might also be open to hearing his viewpoint, since the validity of her emotions has first been supported. On the other hand, if he's having a bad day himself and can't relate to her emotions, her awareness of his style may also save them a big fight. Instead of blaming him for being insensitive, she can remember that he's just more rationally oriented and going through his own tribulations at this moment. He's okay. She's okay. They're just different. Just because he can't relate to her problem this time doesn't mean he doesn't love her and support her. This understanding can save her from escalating the mismatch in emotional styles into a big fight. Furthermore, she can then appeal to his intellect in letting him know, without blame, that they have just had one of their famous rational-versus-emotional miscommunications. Both learn and no one feels bad.

Understanding Your Emotional Style

Be an objective observer this week. When an upsetting situation occurs, in addition to identifying your mind traps, identify how you are relating to the disturbance emotionally. You may also want to try the following exercise on observing your emotions.

Ever thought back on something that happened and then re-experienced the feelings associated with it? For years I was burdened by the memory of a perfectly understandable mistake I made as a teenager. I had gone to a party that got out of hand and the police were called to break it up. No one was arrested, but a friend of mine told her mother what had happened, and in turn that woman told my parents. For years afterward, the memory of that party made me feel ashamed. When I thought about it, my posture would change, my voice would become low, and I would become agitated and angry.

This is the power of the mind. This exercise is designed to help you deal with your mind and the emotions it can generate.

Part 1: Awareness of Negative Emotions

Take a pencil and paper. Write down two or three memories associated with anger. Fill in as much detail as you can. What happened and what was said. Notice how the memories make you feel. Locate the feelings in your body. For instance, some people experience anger as a knot in the stomach, others a burning sensation in the heart and the throat, and others as extreme muscle tension or as other sensations. Record your own reactions. Did the memory of anger bring up other emotions like sadness? How do those feel? Record the following:

- The "memory" emotion. In this case, anger.
- The physical feelings associated with the memory.
- Any other emotions that the memory triggered and their associated bodily feelings.

Repeat the exercise with fear, guilt, shame, sadness, and any other negative emotion you wish to explore.

Part 2: Positive Emotions

Repeat the exercise for love, confidence, joy, peace, or any other positive state. For confidence, write down memories of things you accomplished that made you feel good. They needn't be accomplishments that other people necessarily appreciated. For instance, I can remember the moment I learned to read. First came the struggle of telling an *a* from an *o* and a *p* from a *q*. Then while I was riding in the car one day, suddenly the letters of a sign clicked into a recognizable unity—STOP. What a high!

In the Mind/Body Clinic, we do the preceding exercise in our minds during a meditation period. People often notice that they can readily re-experience some emotions but not others. The ones that can't be retrieved can be powerful clues. It's the rare person who has really mastered anger and learned forgiveness. Repression is the more likely explanation. Take note of which emotions came easily and which were unavailable. What did you *do* with the emotion? Did you express it and learn from it, or did you overexpress, deny, or repress it? Can you think of why that might be? How did people deal with that emotion in your family when you were growing up?

You may or may not be able to get insight about your early conditioning from the exercise. It always helps to share the results with someone who knows you well and may be aware of certain things about your emotional style you can't see. Furthermore, some people relate to such an exercise more easily than others. Just because you may not feel emotions strongly in this exercise doesn't mean that you're a denier. Ask yourself whether your experience in the exercise coincides with real-life reactions.

Patients in the clinic often recognize certain similarities between recalled positive emotions and negative ones. Positive emotions create bodily sensations of openness and expansiveness. They invite the world in. The body feels relaxed, even though some emotions such as joy are very energizing. In contrast, negative emotions create a tight, contracted feeling. Everything pulls inward. The world is pushed away. *Positive feelings invite unity. Negative feelings invite isolation.*

Becoming a skilled observer of your own emotions allows you to make a conscious choice between love and unity or fear and isolation. I am not saying that this skill is easy to develop, only that it is possible and very desirable. At the emotional balance point, the ego takes a back seat. Its wants and fears are not heeded. Instead, we just observe our emotional state with acceptance and interest. Without judging whether we are good or bad, we simply use the intellect to make the discrimination about how best to learn from our own emotional state. Does anger mean that we have to take a particular action, or is an attitudinal shift required instead? What's to be learned from our fear?

Learning from Emotions

By taking the stance of the observer, the Witness who notices without judgment, we can experience negative states without becoming overwhelmed by them. When you notice an upset feeling, zoom in with awareness. Where do you feel it in your body? This is an important step. Perhaps what seems at first like anger is more strongly experienced as hurt. *Give the emotion a name.* What are you really feeling? Then reflect on why you are experiencing it. Keep an eye out for your ego, which will trot out all its mind traps to ensure that you or someone else gets the blame or the praise. The idea is not to end the analysis by finding a culprit but by understanding why you react the way you do, regardless of what happened to provoke the emotion and whether there is justification for feeling it. The truth is that anger doesn't have to be justified for it to be okay to feel angry. All emotions are okay. Without them we wouldn't learn much about ourselves.

Once you have named the emotion and reflected on where it came from, you can then make an informed choice. If it's not important, perhaps you can let it go.

John was a fifty-year-old businessman who had had a heart attack. On his way into a Mind/Body Group meeting, his brand-new Mercedes got dented in the hospital garage. He felt the constriction in his chest, the pounding heart, and the shortness of breath that accompanied his anger and decided that it wasn't worth being angry over a dent. His heart was more important. He took a breath, let go with a sigh of relief, and on the next several out breaths reminded himself to relax further by using the spontaneous mantra "It's not important," "It's not important."

Just take a breath and drop back into the position of the observer—the Witness aspect of the Self that notices without judging. This makes a world of difference in your ability to discriminate whether you can let go or whether some action or attitudinal change is required. Witness consciousness also puts you back in control of your feelings. In a rage the intellect is clouded. You are not a person who is angry, you *are* anger. Remember the story of the boat named RAGE?

The problem with emotions is not that we experience them. Experiencing emotions is necessary for personal growth. It is part of being human. The problem comes either when we get stuck in them and can't let go or when we're not even aware that we have them. The two "stickiest" emotions—the hardest to let go, whether we're holding on consciously or unconsciously—are variants of blame. When we blame ourselves, we feel guilty and ashamed. When we hold on to blaming someone else, we experience resentment. The damage persists long after the situation has passed. Patients often remark that they're still holding on to anger about something someone did years ago. The tragedy is that the anger remains long after any positive learning can come out of it. Some of us are still nursing grudges against people who have been dead for years.

When you think of a person you still resent, you begin to notice the physical effects. The heart speeds up, the stomach churns, and the muscles tense. The person you're burning up over, in the meantime, is going about his business unaffected. This simple truth crops up in aphorisms and stories from all cultures. The Buddha compared holding on to anger to grasping a hot coal with the intent of throwing it at someone else. You, of course, are the one who gets burned. A modern meditation teacher, Swami Chidvilasananda, likens holding on to anger to burning down your house in order to get rid of a rat.

Guilt is a special case of anger. The rat you're burning down your house to exorcise is none other than yourself and it's impossible to run away from yourself. Again, there's nothing wrong with guilt that is dealt with at the moment it occurs. It is a message that we might have done better to make some other choice—to do something differently. The problem comes when we get the message but can't let go of the messenger.

Since guilt makes us feel bad, it often spawns spin-off reactions. The usual response toward someone who hurts you is anger. In guilt you are angry at yourself. That anger can also spill over onto the person you originally considered your victim. Let's say that you have good intentions about visiting a sick aunt in a nursing home. You're busy and time passes. Each time you call her on the phone, she asks when you will come. Pretty soon you are too embarrassed to call her. Finally you begin to resent her for making you feel bad. Once the moment passes for dealing with an emotion simply—either telling the aunt that, regrettably, you can't make it or simply making the time—the hole gets progressively deeper.

Letting Go of Resentment and Guilt

Most of us are carrying around a lot of unnecessary baggage full of guilt and resentment. Even when we're not immediately in touch with it, it affects our behavior nonetheless. I can guarantee you that the owner of the boat named RAGE had a gunny sack full of leftover resentments. The anger spilled out in his aggressive disregard of other boaters. A person who is angry with himself may likewise aggress on others. Often the people who are most critical of other people's behavior are those who are most critical of themselves. Their constant efforts to correct and control those around them add to the burden since their victims are likely to respond with anger and annoyance, perpetuating the cycle.

Before we can let go of resentment, we have to understand why a person who has hurt us did so. Sometimes people are simply unaware of the consequences of their actions. They're not evil—just ignorant. If you don't confront them with the fruits of their ignorance when they hurt you, however, then the opportunity for them to learn may be lost. They are ignorant, but you end up holding on to the resentment. That's not so smart either. Other times people who act hurtfully have themselves been hurt.

Stored patterns of helplessness and rage can play themselves out powerfully. It's hard to break the cycle until the aggressor's own wounds are healed. People don't usually hurt others intentionally. Most hurt comes either from ignorance or from the repetition of unconscious patterns. Most of us are really doing the best we can at any given time. There's little point in looking back in hindsight and whipping yourself because you didn't know then what you know now.

A while back I was driving in my car. When I stopped at a red light, I noticed a boy of about ten hanging out the back window of the station wagon in front of me. He caught my eye, curled his upper lip, and gave me the finger. Instead of giving it back, I thought of all the hurt he must have been feeling to express himself in such a hostile manner. So I just looked into his eyes with all the love I could muster. He responded by breaking into a smile and waving at me until his car drove out of sight.

This is an example of an easy exchange—we didn't know each other. It is harder to see how pain affects the behavior of a person who is closer to you. The following two stories are reframes that are helpful in letting go of anger and seeing the reasons behind things that are not readily apparent.

Reframing Attack as the Need for Love

Robin Casarjian, a therapist who lectures widely on forgiveness, tells a beautiful story about an American aikido student in Japan. Aikido is a form of martial arts that actually teaches balance in life. Students are prohibited from using it against another person unless physical harm is certain.

As Casarjian tells it, further modified by time and my own retellings, an aikido student was riding in a subway one hot summer's day. A drunken, foul-mouthed laborer got on the train and promptly cuffed a young woman, sending her sprawling with her baby. Looking around for a fight, he saw only an old man, an elderly couple, and the young aikido student. The student and the drunken laborer squared off to fight. The student knew that the drunk was no match for him.

Suddenly the little old man tugged on the laborer's clothes, saying he noticed the laborer's enjoyment of drinking. The laborer swore at the old man, who persisted, remarking how he and his wife sipped a bottle of saki each night in their garden as they watched the slow recovery of a little peach tree injured in a storm. The drunk was so astonished that the old man dared talk to him that he began to listen. When the old man asked the drunk whether he had a wife to share saki with, the drunk began to cry, explaining that his own wife had died in childbirth the year before. In his grief he had lost his job and taken to drink. Soon the drunk was resting his head on the frail shoulders of the old man. The old man stroked the drunk's hair and listened with great compassion to his sorrows. The student, who watched this entire scene unfold, understood that he'd seen a true master of aikido at work.

We are told from childhood not to judge another person until we have walked a mile in his shoes. Nonetheless, it's a hard lesson to take to heart. If we could really relate to the other person's pain, then it would be a lot easier to forgive and forget. Dr. Jerry Jampolsky states the essential reframe very well in his powerful book, *Love Is Letting Go of Fear*. In his eyes the attack of another person is best thought of as a cry for help. The attack arises out of the person's own pain. The only remedy for pain is love. We can see this most clearly with children. A tired child gets irritable. Sometimes he attacks us, whining, yelling, or even having a tantrum. Do we attack the child back or realize that he just needs a little love and a nap?

While it is crucial to understand another person's perspective so that we don't have to take attacks so seriously, I am not suggesting that you automatically turn the other cheek. At the moment of attack, when anger comes up in you, exercise your discrimination. If a counterattack is the most creative choice, the event most likely to lead you or the other person to a better understanding, then go for it. On the other hand, if the attack is the kind where letting go is the best choice, it helps to reframe the attacker as needing love right at that moment. In all cases, there is no percentage in holding on to anger after its usefulness is gone.

Reframing the Attacker as the Teacher

Another powerful reframe that helps us let go of resentment is illustrated by the story of a petty tyrant. Author/anthropologist Carlos Castañeda tells the story of an unusually cruel and malicious man who wantonly criticizes, dehumanizes, and physically mistreats his employee, Don Juan, a Mexican wise man whose teachings form the core of Castañeda's books. Don Juan finally escapes from his tormentor, seeking refuge at the home of his teacher. Amazingly, the teacher sends him back. He assures Don Juan that the fastest way to learn inner balance is to return to the cruel employer, staying there until no word or deed can draw him out of his center of strength and peacefulness. Everyone, he says, should hope for the grace of a petty tyrant to teach them this lesson.

I often think of this story when I encounter petty tyrants in my own life. I try to breathe and let go, centering in the inner Witness, not letting someone else's crazy behavior destroy my own peace of mind. Sometimes I succeed, and sometimes I don't, but I always try to feel grateful for the lesson. This has been one of the most helpful reframes for letting go of resentment, as well as for not getting drawn out into an initial angry reaction.

Finishing Old Business

Letting go of resentments and regrets is a way of freeing ourselves from the past. We can only really enjoy the present when all our energy is available to be in the moment rather than tied up in the threads of unfinished business. When I was in college, I got a letter from an old high school sweetheart named Mark that I'll never forget.

We had a rocky relationship. Nothing I did ever seemed to please him. Mark kept professing his love and, like most teenage boys, pressing me for sex, but his behavior was at odds with his words. I was angry and hurt when we broke up. I didn't understand what was wrong with me. In the letter, sent four years after we'd last seen each other, Mark apologized for his actions. He explained that he was in love with another girl who was off at boarding school. I was just a stand-in. Instead of enjoying me for who I was, he rejected me for not being her. Mark was too guilty to tell me what was happening at the time, but it had bothered him for four years. He wanted to say that he was sorry. He wanted to finish his business and let it go. I'll always think well of him for being mature enough to confess his confusion and apologize.

Patients at the Mind/Body Clinic who are members of Alcoholics Anonymous are already familiar with this principle. One of the twelve steps in that program—the guiding principles through which they can conquer their addiction—involves taking a "fearless" inventory of the wrongs they have committed. Then they apologize to the person or persons involved and do their best to make amends. The little voice inside that berates them for being a bad person can then stop its litany of blame.

You can use the same principle to let go of resentment. Write a letter telling the person exactly what he or she did and why you are still angry. Some people write such letters without mailing them. It still helps to get the feelings off your chest. Others find that mailing the letter seems the better choice. If you do mail the letter, don't be attached to the results. The other person may not acknowledge the situation or may return new anger. On the other hand, he or she may take the opportunity to apologize to you. In any case, this is your show, your chance to finish your business regardless of how the other person reacts.

During my work with critically ill patients, I've noticed that many have a spontaneous desire to finish old business. For example, one of my patients named Bob, an engineer in his mid-thirties, was dying from acute leukemia. He had called his ex-wife while in the hospital and requested that she fly from New York to see him. They had a warm and moving afternoon, releasing each other from the blame and guilt that often surround relationships that have ended. He repeated this exercise with his father, his brother, and an old boss. He described the process as casting the stones over the side of his hot-air balloon so that he'd be free to float to heaven. Impending death makes the need to finish personal business very pressing. It's too bad that we don't consider living our lives in peace and openness to love to be as pressing a reason for clearing the past.

The Meaning of Forgiveness

Forgiveness is a charged word. Everybody has a different opinion about what it means. To some it is a religious commandment that sounds okay in theory but is difficult to execute in practice. It calls forth images of Jesus dying on the cross, looking compassionately at his tormentors as he prays, "Forgive them, Father, for they know not what they do." Some people relate very positively to this image. To others it seems like abdicating responsibility, becoming a victim.

There's another understanding of forgiveness that is both theoretically sound and practically feasible. It is consistent with any belief system, secular or religious. *Forgiveness means accepting the core of every human being as the same as yourself and giving them the gift of not judging them.* You can be clear about whether or not a person's behavior is acceptable without judging the person. Psychologists caution parents never to criticize their child, only the child's behaviors. "You are stupid" is a very different statement from "Your behavior is not acceptable to me." If a person knows that you respect and value him or her, your comments about behavior are welcome. If you are attacking the person's character, however, no comment, no matter how perceptive, will be heeded. Forgiveness starts with ourselves and extends to others. Accepting that the core of your own being is as precious and wonderful as that of any other person is the greatest gift you can ever give yourself.

Learn to love yourself now, not later. Even if you haven't lost twenty pounds, finished cleaning the house, become chairman of your department, or won a Nobel Prize, you are still okay. Sometimes my patients tell me that they want to be like me. I ask them what's wrong with being like them? I might have enjoyed being like Mozart, but the fact is that I am totally devoid of musical talent. I can spend the rest of my life judging my musical deficiencies, or I can realize that it's great to be who I am. The world is filled with diversity. That's what makes it so wonderful.

When Myrin and I got married, we exchanged a very meaningful vow. We gave each other a red rose, promising that we would set each other free to follow the God within. This is forgiveness. I am free to be me. He is free to be himself. It took about fourteen years to really understand and enact that vow, but every minute of the struggle has been worthwhile. We can now truly appreciate each other's uniqueness—at least most of the time!

Perhaps the most moving personal descriptions of forgiveness and self-acceptance come from the studies of psychologist Dr. Kenneth Ring. In his book *Heading Toward Omega*, he writes about the meaning of near-death experiences to people who have them. (It is notable that a poll by George

Gallup, Jr., indicates that one in twenty adult Americans has had a near-death experience. Even this figure may be an underestimate since many people are afraid to share their experience for fear of being ridiculed.)

Ring found that the near-death experience, while variable, has a common set of events. It begins with a sensation of incredible peace and well-being, perceived as overwhelming joy and happiness. There is no pain or indeed any awareness of bodily sensation. The person reports floating free of the body, observing it and the conversations around it in a detached manner. Everything seems very real and natural, not like a dream or a hallucination. At some point the person becomes aware of another "reality" and the presence of a being of light that radiates total acceptance, compassion, and love. The descriptions of the light are awe-inspiring. At some point, the being stimulates a life review that happens almost instantaneously. As one person describes the experience in Ring's book:

> . . . it was not my life that passed in front of me nor was it a three-dimensional caricature of the events in my life. What occurred was every emotion I have ever felt in my life, I felt. And my eyes were showing me the basis of how that emotion affected my life. What my life had done so far to affect other people's lives using the feeling of pure love that was surrounding me as the point of comparison.

Another survivor of a near-death experience explains:

> You are shown your life—and you do the judging. . . . It's the little things—maybe a hurt child that you helped or just to stop to say hello to a shut-in. Those are the things that are most important. . . . You have been forgiven all your sins, but are you able to forgive yourself for not doing the things you

should have done and some little cheaty things that maybe you've done in life? Can you forgive yourself? This is the judgment.

The experience unfolds to reveal a reality where everyone is in a state of absolute compassion for everyone else. Love is the major focus. In that state everything makes sense. The pain and suffering of life fall into place and judgment drops away; only compelling love, warmth, and total acceptance remain. Many of those who have a near-death experience are reluctant to go back to life as we know it but understand that they must, that there are still necessary things to be accomplished. Some of the most startling descriptions, however, revolve around what they consider necessary. Most people report that the accomplishments they had thought most important—in their work, for instance—were of no importance at all. It was the amount of love they shared—expressed in even the smallest ways—that was the most meaningful accomplishment of a lifetime.

People who have near-death experiences often report that they have become much more forgiving of others—they no longer judge. Instead, their primary orientation turns toward love and acceptance of themselves and others. The entire meaning of life is reframed. The challenge to the 95 percent of us who have not had such an experience is clear. *Practice forgiveness by recognizing the perfect inner core of yourself and other people.* If you are not religious, you can think of it as recognizing that the same basic consciousness—whatever its ultimate nature—is present in every person. Only the individuality of our life experiences creates the sense that we are separate. If you are religious, follow the core teaching of every great religion. The message of the Christian tradition is "Love your Father first, and love your neighbor as yourself." The message that can be distilled from Eastern traditions is "God dwells within you as you." Therefore, see God in one another.

✥ Suggestions for the Reader

1. Familiarize yourself with your emotional style. The exercise on observing your emotions should be helpful.

2. Accept your emotions as human. Remember that the only negative emotions are those you push away, since you are then deprived of the learning they can stimulate.

3. Deal with your emotions as they happen; don't store them up. To do this:
   - Give the emotion a name.
   - Take a breath and step back to the position of the observer.
   - Consider why you are feeling that way.
   - Reflect on what you *did* with the emotion. Did you express it, overexpress it, deny it, or repress it? Or did you learn from it, allowing it to become a healing force in your life?
   - Choose the most skillful course of action:
     To let go
     To reframe and seek a new understanding
     To take a specific, necessary action

4. Finish your unfinished business. Make a list of the regrets and resentments that you are holding on to. Be fiercely honest with yourself. It's too easy to think you've let something go when you haven't. Do what it takes to finish your business. Make phone calls, write letters, whether you mail them or not. Apologize and make amends where appropriate for things that you're sorry for. Tell people how you really feel.

5. Practice forgiveness. Let go of your judgments and give yourself and others the gift of being who they are, accepting them for what they are instead of rejecting them for not fitting your expectations.

6. Honor your own Self and honor the Self in others. The Eastern greeting *Namaste* is similar in meaning to Hebrew and Hawaiian greetings. It means "The Self in me honors and salutes the Self in you."

8

Sam's Story

The radical growth in medical science and technology over the last fifty years has redefined the expectations of doctors and patients. Before the discovery of antibiotics, it was common for children and young adults to die of infection. Physicians often had little to give other than safe, caring passage through the natural course of a disease.

By comparison, modern physicians can work wonders. Now that most acute illness is under control, chronic disease has become the more common problem. Even heart disease, cancer, and diabetes can be controlled, often for extended periods. Nonetheless, the final outcome for all of us remains unchanged. Eventually we will all die. Where death was once viewed as a natural part of life, it has now grown remote and is often seen as a failure on the part of medicine to work its miracles. Death has become the enemy.

Many patients come to me facing the uncertainty of whether they can be cured or even if death can be held at bay. Curiously, this frame of mind can lead to a healing of attitudes that might otherwise have come more slowly or perhaps not at all. When familiar frames of reference are shattered by the nearness of death, new understanding can evolve rapidly.

Some of the most profound experiences of my life have come through working with exceptional people who use death to come to a greater understanding of the wholeness of life. One such experience of healing that inspires me every day is the story of Sam. The healing was both Sam's and my own. We met in the late winter of 1983 when the psychiatry department at Beth Israel Hospital called me in for a consultation. Sam, a young physician in his thirties, had just learned that he had AIDS. He was hospitalized with *Pneumocytis carinii* pneumonia, an infection often associated with AIDS. In his agitation and sadness, Sam had asked whether anyone in the hospital taught meditation, since he thought it could help him achieve peace of mind.

Since Sam's story is a very personal one, it is best told as it occurred, largely through the conversations between us during the year that we worked together. As in other stories, I have changed dates, names, and details to protect the identity of Sam and his loved ones.

As I set out for this "peace of mind" consult, I wanted to get through it quickly because it was beginning to snow and I had a long drive home. I thought of waiting until morning, but then I put myself in Sam's place. He was waiting for help.

When I arrived at Sam's door, it was plastered with precaution signs—specific instructions about handling blood products and bodily secretions and excretions. There was a cart containing sterile gowns, gloves, and face masks outside the door.

The masks were actually for the patient's protection, in case a staff member had a respiratory infection. Even a cold could prove fatal to someone in such a weakened condition. As I put on a gown, I lingered in my preparations, wondering what to expect. I was scared. Not so much about contagion, but scared that I couldn't help someone in such a terrible circumstance. I took a deep breath and at last was ready to go in.

The room was semi-dark. A nurse was moving Sam's intravenous line. Dozens of cards lined the walls. The late winter sun cast long shadows across the room. Sam was lying under the covers, pale and shaking, his wet blond hair plastered against his forehead.

I stood in the doorway for a moment, collecting my thoughts. Was he contagious after all? AIDS was still a recent phenomenon, and medical science had not yet begun to unravel its secrets. Not even the virus had been isolated. I thought of Myrin and our children and wondered if I should be here. Just then Sam opened his eyes and saw me. He smiled and extended his hand from under the blankets. "You're Dr. Borysenko, aren't you?" I moved to his side, smiled and reached for his hand. He thanked me for coming and, in a weak voice, began to tell his story.

Sam had been ill for about six months. At first his physician had thought that he had hepatitis. In spite of months of bed rest, he had not grown better; he had developed a bad case of thrush, a fungus infection, and began to suspect that he had AIDS. The pneumonia clinched the diagnosis. We spoke of how he might have contracted the disease and of his feelings about it. He was gay and had a good relationship. His lifestyle in no way reflected the stereotype of the first AIDS patients. His openness, dignity, and hopefulness, even in the face of people's fear and misunderstandings about the disease, were exceptional.

I asked Sam why he had called me in. At first he spoke scientifically, about the effect of stress on the immune system and how he had concluded that the relaxation response might reduce his stress and give his immune system the best chance of recovery. This was Sam's intellectualization, but his real feelings came out quite quickly. As we talked, he gripped my hand more tightly and began to cry.

Then he said, "All my life, I've searched for meaning in the things I could accomplish. I became a physician—a good one. I felt I was a good son, a good friend, that I worked hard to establish a relationship. I've spent my life getting secure, acquiring the things we all think of as important. A house, a car, enough money to do the things I want." He paused to cough and catch his breath, then he propped himself on an elbow and continued in a soft voice. "I've spent a lot of time in therapy, too, trying to understand myself, but somehow all those things don't seem to be enough. Part of me is empty, longing for something. I don't seem to have any peace. That's why I asked for you. Is there really some way to experience peace of mind?"

The room was perfectly still, other than the relentless clicking of the IV machine that delivered the antibiotics that were fighting off Sam's pneumonia. I thought of that long string of zeros my teacher had spoken of and of my own search for meaning and peace. I wondered if I was up to this challenge. How could I help Sam when I wasn't sure I had the answers myself?

In spite of the doubt, my words came out with a certainty that riveted us both. "I can't teach you, because you already have peace inside. But I can remind you of how to experience that feeling again." We were both silent, gazing intently at each other. Only a few times in my life have I had such a deeply connected experience with another human being. We trusted each other immediately and completely, and that trust was to take us both beyond our ordinary understanding of life.

I explained the basics of meditation to Sam. He wanted a focus word that reminded him of the inner peace he was searching for. He settled on the breath mantra, *Ham Sah,* and we had a few minutes of meditation. The silence was broken by his nurse, who came in to check his vital signs and adjust the IV. She commented on how much better he was looking.

It was getting late, and the last rays of daylight had long passed. The Boston skyline was breathtaking from Sam's large window, particularly against the backdrop of falling snow. Sam looked at me with a special, tender smile—a smile that I returned. We made a plan for me to check on him the following morning before my clinic hours began.

I thought of Sam all the way home. How strange life could be. Here I had just spent an hour with a young man who was fighting a deadly disease, and yet I was not depressed. I hadn't felt so peaceful for a long time.

The next day I arrived at the hospital to find Sam much improved. The antibiotics were taking effect and he was sitting up in bed. He had already done a morning meditation, and he asked me the usual questions about the wandering mind. We soon began to talk of Sam's favorite hobby, downhill skiing. He told me he was aware of how quiet his mind became when he concentrated on the body feelings, the balance and dexterity, that skiing demands. Just remembering the experience of speed and control brought a look of peacefulness to his face. He told me that he understood that peacefulness is the constant background that is re-experienced whenever the mind slows down. We sat quietly for a while, both pondering the times that we had really felt peace. Just as I was reliving a curious, long-forgotten childhood memory, Sam's voice roused me from my reverie.

"Can the mind stop during intense fear, do you think? If you are totally riveted in fright, can the experience actually flip over into peacefulness?" How strange that he had asked.

The question related intimately to the early memory I had recalled, so I began to talk about it.

When I was about three or four years old, my father and I were playing in a swimming pool. He was a porpoise and I was a mermaid riding on his back. I suddenly slipped and sucked in my breath in fear as I slid sideways off his back. Then the fear was suddenly gone. I was floating upside down in the water, enjoying how the filtered sunlight played and danced in the water, how every ripple shimmered with light. The body of a swimmer passed above, setting up amazing currents in the water. In the meantime I had forgotten to be afraid. The sudden surprise of finding myself in such an enchanting world had completely stopped my mind.

Sam was shaking his head, quickly making associations between my story and a book his lover, David, had been reading to him, Kenneth Ring's *Heading Toward Omega*. Sam was amazed that although people who have had near-death experiences all have different perceptions, there is still a common experience. "For example," he said, "in a matter of seconds your entire life replays. Isn't time perception strange? It's incredible to think that the brain could replay so much information in a way that is consciously meaningful in what must be literally seconds."

"Mmm," I broke in. "I've thought a lot about that too. Meditation really points up the relativity of time. Sometimes ten minutes seem like an hour, and other times an hour seems to pass in a minute. Einstein said, when you're sitting on a hot stove, two minutes seem like two hours, but when you're in the arms of your beloved, two hours seem like two minutes. Isn't it true?"

We both laughed and then Sam continued, shifting his position and encircling his legs with his arms so that he could rest his chin on his knees. He was gazing off into space. "After their life is replayed before them," he continued, "people relate seeing some sort of tunnel, which feels very appealing. On the other end of the tunnel they emerge into a peaceful, totally accepting light, which they instantly recognize as unconditional love. It's like your swimming pool experience. They don't get scared, don't get into some rap about what they're missing back at the ranch, they just surrender to the incredible love, peace, and beauty. At this point the experience gets variable. People may see deceased family members or different saints and religious figures. There then follows some sort of recognition or communication that it's not time to go yet, and they are transported back through the tunnel and into their bodies."

I sighed, about to tell Sam a story about a scientist I'd met a few months earlier, but I changed my mind. I wanted to know more from him first. "What do you think about those accounts, Sam? Do they make any sense to you? "

He nodded. "I think so. On the other hand, I remember reading an article from *Psychology Today* a few years ago that tried to reduce those experiences to some preprogrammed trick of dying brain cells. Some way that we could die in peace. Even if that's true, though, it's hard to attribute such a great design—the last video game of the show—to chance. I would have to believe that such an exceptional program was created by some intelligent, loving force, and then the point becomes moot. We're talking about God either way, so why invent theories? If some people have actually experienced this, I want to learn more. It certainly challenges my ideas about what death is."

We looked at each other and said in unison, "And what life is." We both giggled in relief. It broke the spell for a moment, and I got up to stretch and examine the magnificent arrangement of anthuriums, shiny red, heart-shaped flowers with a waxy appearance, that rested on a table by Sam's window. I remembered seeing them on a trip to Hawaii, where they grew in great profusion. I'd had an anthurium plant for years as well, and it had actually bloomed from time to time. The resemblance of the blooms to hearts seemed to capture the mood of the moment. Sam and I discussed his brother, who had sent the arrangement. He had so many good friends and such a supportive family.

"You started to say something a few minutes ago when we were discussing near-death experiences," Sam said. "What was it?"

I had to pause. I rarely venture into the realm of the spiritual with patients, and it made me uncomfortable. I am a therapist, not a minister. We discussed my feelings and concluded that the work Sam and I were engaged in was different from traditional therapy. We were both teachers and both learners. I decided to see Sam on my own time rather than as a patient. Then it felt okay to continue with my story.

I began to recount a trip to a scientific conference where I had met a leading immunologist named Dan. The meeting was a seemingly chance occurrence in the hotel coffee shop before the morning sessions began. It was very crowded, and people had begun doubling up at tables. When Dan sat down, we introduced ourselves and said a few words about what we did. When he heard that I had an interest in mind/body interactions and in exploring the mind through psychology and meditation, he became pensive. He then asked permission to tell me a story that had been deeply disturbing to him. Dan still didn't know what to make of it and thought that perhaps I could help.

Several months earlier Dan had been hospitalized with acute abdominal pain, and a number of tests had been ordered. He had been given a narcotic to ease the pain and apparently had a bad reaction to it. His body got hot and restless. Dan then began to feel strangely energized and had the odd and compelling sensation of rising up to the top of his head and exiting through a hole near the back of his skull. He described the sensation with wide eyes and a sense of wonder.

"I—that is, the thinking, sentient part of me, what I would label as my identity—rose up out of my body. I hovered around the ceiling, looking down on the sweaty body below, as if I were seeing it in the movies. I remember noticing how filthy the top of the moldings were and making a note to tell the nurse later. In the meantime I overheard them discussing my case in the hall. I simply floated through the wall, without even noting it as a barrier, and observed the conversation. I clearly perceived that the internist was preoccupied with family problems and that I was not going to get the care I needed from him. I was sure of it. Don't ask me how. I just knew, clearly and absolutely. In that moment I also had a strong impression of what was causing my problem. I was having referred pain from a kidney infection that had nothing to do with my GI tract. At that moment I felt a strong pull back to my body and had the sensation of slipping back in through the back of my skull.

"Then I made the mistake of trying to discuss my experience with the internist. He wanted to put me on tranquilizers. He thought I'd had a hallucination caused by the drug and called the psychiatry department for a consult. Meanwhile I got up, got dressed, kidnapped my chart, and called a cab, leaving the hospital AMA—against medical advice. I had the cab drop me at a hospital across town, where I knew one of the internists on the staff. As luck would have it, he was on call when I arrived. I explained my hunch to him, and it proved correct. I did not explain how I came to have the hunch, since I don't think most people will believe me."

I had been listening with rapt attention, wondering why he was telling all this to me—a complete stranger. Bernie Siegel explains such apparently serendipitous phenomena with the quip that coincidence is merely God's way of remaining anonymous. Perhaps so. I asked Dan how he felt about the experience—whether it had changed his ideas about himself. He laughed and said,

"That's the understatement of the century. There's no way anymore for me to assume that I'm just a body. The body was more like a suit of clothes that I slipped out of at the end of the day. The essential me was independent of the body. Of that much I am absolutely sure. Beyond that, I don't know what to think, other than I need to know more."

We went on to discuss descriptions from the spiritual literature and the literature on near-death experiences that paralleled his hospital story. Although many people have had similar experiences, like Dan they learn not to discuss them. It was very important for him to learn that he was not alone.

When I finished Dan's story I said to Sam, "We ended up having a conversation very similar to the one you and I have been having. Sometimes I wonder. For sure I don't have the answers to these things, and yet the question about what is mind, what is body, what is spirit seems to come up at every turn. It's quite confusing. Anyway, I told Dan to read Gary Zukov's book, *The Dancing Wu Li Masters*, about the new physics and consciousness. You might enjoy it too." I paused, reflecting on my long search for meaning in life. "Here we go again, back to the scientist trying to understand the spirit. It all seems beyond science, yet physicists do such a good job of bringing the mind up against limits that can be hurdled only by going beyond concepts."

I was feeling a little sheepish about going on for so long, but Sam just looked at me and said something that brought tears to my eyes—something I will always remember. With great tenderness, he said, "Your children must really love you." My story was meant for his mind, but it had penetrated his heart.

There was often a very timeless, peaceful quality to our meetings, as on this occasion. At other times the talk was of immediate problems, of the reality of his illness. Of all the diseases that I've seen people cope with, AIDS is the most difficult. Because it is often sexually transmitted, and because it began largely in the homosexual population, it has brought out some people's worst fears and insecurities. People who are preoccupied with the idea of a punitive God imagine AIDS to be a divine punishment. Having to cope with such narrow-minded fear is an additional burden for the AIDS patient. Yet even this additional burden can lead to new understandings because it often helps people with AIDS to review their own religious beliefs, taking stock of their lives and beginning or continuing to explore their ideas about life.

Another difficulty the AIDS patient must cope with is the unpredictability of the physical course of the disease. Some people remain relatively well for a prolonged period. Others suffer many illnesses and setbacks, dying very quickly. Because of its unpredictability, AIDS brings up all the issues we have about being in control and all the helplessness that is born out of the feeling that the disease has pulled out the rug. Loss of weight is common, leading to a dramatic change in body image. Sam's case was compounded by the appearance of Kaposi's sarcoma, a cancer that is rare in anyone other than those with seriously weakened immunity, such as AIDS patients. The dark purplish tumors spread over Sam's face and upper body early in the disease, serving as a constant reminder of the gravity of his condition. Many of our talks zeroed in on Sam's mourning for the health and for the opportunities he had lost. Many of our meetings were hardly talks at all—just periods of sitting together, mostly quiet.

Sam stayed in the hospital for two weeks. On his last day, I visited him just before he was to leave. He looked great, dressed in a blue athletic suit and a pair of white sneakers. What a difference, compared to the white hospital gown. He looked like a person, not a patient. I realize that he would be bouncing between those identities in very painful ways during the coming months.

As we talked, Sam described how quickly his emotions changed. One moment he was lost in an emotional wilderness of fear. The next he was lifted into a consideration of immortality—lifted by a profound sense that God is the living consciousness of love and that even AIDS is part of the plan, an opportunity to break down limits and build bridges back to God. I remember feeling a real identification with what he said. One minute everything made sense; it seemed like grace. The next I would wonder if it wasn't all some sort of delusion.

As we shared our experience of the past two weeks, I told him about the fascinating theories of Belgian physicist Ilya Prigogine, who won the Nobel Prize in 1977. I remember from high school physics that the universe is supposedly running downhill, according to the second law of thermodynamics. In other words, order necessarily degenerates into chaos. In case I should doubt this, I need only look in my sons' bedrooms for proof! I also remember from high school that living systems fly in the face of this law, since more complex systems are always evolving. Prigogine showed that the stimulus for creating order out of disorder is exactly the opposite of what you might imagine. It's actually throwing a monkey wrench into the works that stimulates the creation of new structures at an atomic level and new meanings at a personal level.

Prigogine's theory of "dissipative structures" states that small perturbations in a system may be damped out, kind of swamped by the status quo, so that no real change is produced. But if the monkey wrench is big enough, if the perturbation is strong enough, the system can't absorb the shock. At this point, an opening is created for the whole structure to undergo a startling change, an evolution that he calls an "escape to a higher order." AIDS is surely a big monkey wrench.

After Sam went home, we stayed in touch by phone and met occasionally at restaurants or at his home. During the three hospitalizations he had over the year, we saw each other most intensively. He developed a serious herpes infection one time. Then he had a second bout of pneumonia, which caused great concern, since many AIDS patients don't have the reserve to fight the illness a second time. On the last occasion, Sam battled an intestinal infection. He also had a host of other medical problems, not the least of which were the side effects from the drug interferon. He was always at the ready to fight for his life. He loved life. No matter how long the odds on a treatment, he'd try it. He figured that even if it didn't help him, something of value might be learned for the benefit of others.

During the fall, after Sam had been ill for several months, Steve Maurer and I decided to offer a special mind/body group exclusively for AIDS patients. Sam's plight—with the new understandings it had created—was very moving. I wanted to help others in the same situation. Some of my colleagues expressed concern that I was becoming too involved with this problem. They feared that I might be risking infection by repeated contact with a whole group of AIDS patients. I discussed this with Myrin and Steve Maurer, who had recently joined me in helping to run the mind/body groups and who planned to co-lead the group of AIDS patients. Steve agreed that there are times in life when, after checking the data, you have to trust your gut for the final decision. Both of us felt that the risk of infection was negligible.

Running the group proved to be exceptionally difficult. Emotions were raw. The men were often angry and terribly sad, and many were desperately ill. Ten men started in the group. By the third week four had been hospitalized with various infections or were too ill to come. Each week was a testimony to the frailty of human flesh and to the hope of the human spirit. Any problems that Steve and I had in our lives seemed of little consequence compared to what these men were enduring.

Our group ran for eight weeks, until near the end of winter. In the seventh week, Larry, the seemingly healthiest member, was hospitalized with severe pneumonia. Larry was a truly delightful human being. He always had a joke and a smile. Deeply committed to social change, he was active in the community. Larry also had been deeply interested in spiritual life for several years and shared his thoughts about it openly in the group. It was hard to believe that he had AIDS. His weight was stable, he was still working, and he looked great. With his positive attitude, we all hoped that Larry would be an exception to the grim statistics. So Sam's call one Monday morning, to tell me that Larry was in the intensive care unit with pneumonia, came as a real shock.

Sam's voice broke as he said, "Joan, I want to come to the hospital and be with him. He's so sick, they think he's not going to make it. He's on a respirator. He can't talk. His brother told me that he was scared to death when they brought him in. They tried to page you, but you were away for the weekend. I want to be with him and hold his hand. I want to tell him not to be afraid."

Sam sobbed and sobbed, dissolving in grief at the other end of the telephone. Larry's illness had developed so fast. I was speechless. I had refused to contemplate that either Larry or Sam would actually die, that inevitably that bridge would have to be crossed. I struggled to hold back my tears.

"Sam," I spoke softly, "I know how much you hurt, how much you love Larry and how deeply you care, but you can't go into the intensive care unit. The air is full of Pneumocystis bacteria. You can't expose yourself like that."

Sam continued to weep on the other end of the phone as if his heart would break. AIDS had deprived him of his health; now it had robbed him of the chance to bring comfort to his friend. His tears were for Larry, for himself, and for all the losses that human beings must suffer.

We made a plan for me to go to the intensive care unit to bring Sam's solace and love to Larry. Sam would come to my office later in the afternoon, and then we planned to meditate together.

The short walk to the intensive care unit was difficult—I was feeling so much pain. I stopped at the nurse's station to find out what room Larry was in. On the desk was a small lighted Christmas tree, a symbol that seemed particularly empty at the moment. I stepped into Larry's room totally unprepared for what I saw. He was being artificially breathed by a respirator, connected by a tube in his windpipe. Larry's lungs had stopped working. The machine made a repetitive hissing noise that mixed with the sound of a beautiful chant coming from a tape recorder on the opposite side of the room. I learned later that his brother had requested that the nurses play his favorite chant continuously to help Larry remain peaceful.

Larry's eyes were open and glassy. His lips were parched and dry. A drug had been administered that paralyzed him so his own breathing could not interfere with the action of the respirator. It was all I could do to hold myself together. I had to keep reminding myself that this was Larry's body—not Larry.

It was impossible to tell if he was conscious or not, since he was paralyzed by the drug. Even if he was unconscious, though, I knew that he could hear me. Many patients anesthetized for surgery later recount conversations that occurred in the operating room. I pulled up a chair and sat close to his head. I picked up his stiff, swollen hand and stroked it.

I couldn't talk at first, I was too upset. I said a brief prayer and centered myself with a short meditation. Then I told Larry of Sam's message—how meaningful their relationship was, and how much strength Sam had derived from Larry's talking about his fears, hopes, and spiritual beliefs. Then I told Larry about Elisabeth Kübler-Ross, the psychiatrist who has written about death and dying. She had toured an abandoned Nazi death camp and was particularly horrified at the prospect of seeing the rooms where children had been housed prior to their extermination. She expected to see signs of fear and hatred, but instead the walls were scratched with pictures of butterflies—symbols of the spirit.

I talked of Larry's favorite subject—God's love and grace—and I talked of fear. His, mine, Sam's. I said I hoped that he had gone through the door of fear and entered the space of peace; I was thinking of my own experience at the bottom of the swimming pool so many years before. I couldn't continue. I cried openly. Then I sat silently listening to the strange harmony of the chant and the respirator for quite a long time. I felt more and more peaceful. I was convinced that Larry was at peace.

Sam was waiting for me in my office when I returned. I related the visit. We held on to each other and cried quietly for a little while. Steve came in at that point, and the three of us meditated together. It was very peaceful. Sam emerged with the same feeling I had had—that Larry was doing fine. As Sam got up to leave, I noticed that he was wearing the same blue jogging suit in which he had left the hospital after his first bout with pneumonia the winter before. He looked very tired, and he was unsteady on his feet. I helped him down the elevator and out of the building into a waiting cab. We shivered in the cold December wind, knowing how tenuous life was.

Sam grew progressively weaker, and a chronic bowel infection made his weight loss even more severe. He was hospitalized for the last time in the early spring, just a little more than a year after we had met. Sam's energy was low, and he was often confused. He was also scared.

Late one Thursday afternoon I stopped in to see him on my way out of the hospital. He looked like a child, huddled in bed, clutching the blankets around him. He started to weep when he saw me, telling me how hard it was, particularly the long nights. Even with the support of a dear friend who stayed with him all through the night, his fear was intense. He kept pointing to his heart, talking of a terrible constriction in his chest. "It's like all the fear that I've been holding on to throughout my life is trying to leave all at once. My fear of intimacy, of not being good enough, of everything, I want to let it all go. I hope I can let it all go." He looked at me with such longing. At first I didn't know what to say.

Then I remembered a yantra—a visual focus for meditation—that I had first encountered as the insignia of a Christian spiritual group with which Myrin and I had studied for several years. It is a square within which is a circle. Inside the circle is a triangle, and within that there is a cross. Variants of this symbol are used by many groups, including Alcoholics Anonymous and a number of medical groups who use the adaptation drawn by Leonardo da Vinci—a man standing in the shape of a cross in the center, juxtaposed on the form of a man with legs and arms outstretched like triangles. The man stands within the circle which, in turn, is encased within a square. Such forms that show up in many cultures are examples of archetypes; they carry a meaning that is transcendent of cultural limitations. That yantra is a universal symbol of the Self. Without explanation, I drew it for Sam with a magic marker on the back of a paper plate and told him just to look at it, to let it draw him in when the fear got strong in the night.

Early Friday morning I went to see Sam. He looked much calmer. He told me the yantra had had a soothing effect. Sam said his family was gathering to see him since they knew the end was near. He asked me to come to the hospital on Sunday to be with them. I was deeply touched to be considered part of his family.

Friday night I was terribly restless and began to prowl through my house like a cat. I rummaged through my drawers to locate an old medallion in the shape of the yantra that I'd drawn for Sam. I finally discovered it in an old jewelry box. It was scratched and pitted with age.

I sat for a long time that night, holding the medallion and wondering how people managed to keep their faith in a world so full of suffering. My own faith seemed to come and go like the tide. It had been strong when I was a child and then had faded into the distance during adolescence, only to return more strongly than ever shortly after I met Myrin. After some years of faith, again it faded into a thicket of doubts. It was at a low point before I met Sam. In the late evening hours, I said a prayer for Sam, for me, for all of us. Then I tucked the medallion into my wallet and went to sleep.

Sunday morning dawned clear and crisp. It was one of those sweet, early spring mornings that make you remember how long the winter is. The air smelled like earth, and purple-tipped crocuses were peaking out through the wood chips by the front walk. Spring was Sam's favorite season, and he loved the crocuses and azaleas.

The car was cozy and warm. The snow tires were still on, and they made a familiar humming noise that was quite comforting. As I drove to the hospital I became absorbed in Sam's story, thinking about the changes in both of us over the past year. This had been a year of admitting some of my own fears. Despite all my accomplishments, I was still insecure deep inside. I had perfected an outer mask that was so convincing that sometimes I lost touch with what was underneath. Being with Sam had forced me to resolve my own crisis of faith and renewed my connection to the Inner Self. Sam had been a bridge for me, as I had been one for him. As all these thoughts and feelings filled my mind, the old spiritual, "Amazing Grace," came up from inside. I started to sing it over and over until I reached the hospital.

In the waiting room of the intensive care unit, where Sam had been moved on Saturday, I met his brother and sister-in-law. They told me that he was losing ground fast, but that he was still conscious. We all went into the room together, joining his parents and David, along with two or three close friends. Sam was pale. He looked very small, dwarfed by a huge bank of heart-monitoring equipment. A unit of blood slowly dripped into one arm. The contents of several IV bottles dripped into the other. He reached out to me as I approached his bed, and I leaned down to give him a hug. Then I remembered the medallion tucked away in my wallet. I wanted it to rest over his heart, but I had forgotten to bring a chain. One of his friends found some string, and we improvised a necklace. I bent down and gently placed it around his neck. With his eyes closed, Sam reached down for the medallion and held it for a moment. Then the most remarkable thing happened. He opened his eyes and smiled, then asked me to sing "Amazing Grace."

I was thunderstruck. It was only my shock that allowed me to overcome the embarrassment of being asked to sing that spiritual in a room full of semi-strangers. I knew I had to let that go. As I sang, each word took on a world of meaning. When I got to the verse "Through many dangers, toils and snares I have already come, 'Twas Grace that brought me safe this far, 'Tis Grace shall lead me home," I felt a peace inside like nothing I have ever experienced before. At moments when my faith wavers, I have only to recall that moment. The room was completely silent when I finished, and Sam invited the group to join in a short meditation.

When the meditation was over, Sam did an extraordinary thing. One by one, he called the most meaningful people in his life over to his bedside. Then he just spoke from his heart. He told them how much he loved them; he asked for their forgiveness for whatever pain he might have caused, and he forgave them in the same way. There are no words to express the feelings in my heart as I watched this incredible act of healing and grace.

When Sam was finished, he lay back to rest, and David played tapes of Sam's favorite music. Family and friends came in and out of the room, reminiscing, crying, talking to Sam and one another all afternoon. I was surprised when the voice of Leontyne Price came forth from a tape, singing "Amazing Grace." I had not known that it was one of Sam's favorite songs.

Toward evening it was time to head home. I kissed Sam goodbye for the last time. The next few days I kept in touch with the hospital by telephone since I was away on business. Sam grew progressively weaker, until he died at noon that Wednesday in his father's arms.

The memorial service was scheduled for the following week. David had put together an extremely moving service of music and spiritual readings that captured the essence of Sam. I was to hear it months later on tape, since I was in New Orleans on the day of the service. I was very disappointed not to be there. The evening of the service, Myrin and I were wandering through the narrow streets of the French Quarter. As we turned right on a dimly lit side street,

I caught sight of a saxophonist in a doorway. He followed us with his eyes, as we walked toward him. Slowly raising the instrument to his lips, he closed his eyes and began to play "Amazing Grace."

A few weeks after Sam's death, I met one of his closest friends for lunch, a woman who had been an invaluable and loving support to him throughout his illness. She presented me with a small package, a gift from Sam's family. I couldn't imagine what it might be. I unwrapped the package, lifted the cardboard cover, and found a blue velvet box of the type that usually contains jewelry. I still had no inkling of what lay inside.

As I lifted the cover, a ray of sunlight caught the corner of a square gold object that shone for a moment as bright as the sun. It was the yantra. The family had had it cast in gold. Even as I type this, tears come once again to my eyes. Like the medallion, my faith had been made new. I had been renewed just as surely as had Sam.

The occasion was made complete by the day on which I received that renewed symbol of the Self. It was Good Friday. The crucifixion and the resurrection are not just a story that occurred two thousand years ago. They are archetypes of the ongoing story of mankind, of breaking down the walls and building the bridges that connect each of us to our own inner being—however we may experience that inner divinity—and each of us to one another. This is healing in its most complete sense.

Epilogue

Putting It All Together:
Twelve Brief Reminders

1. **You cannot control the external circumstances of your life, but you can control your reactions to them.**

In trying circumstances, remember your choices:

(a) Reframe the situation as a challenge rather than a threat. In this way you acknowledge and nourish your own inner strength, even as you face doubt and uncertainty. Adversity is the crucible in which the spirit is forged.

(b) Your breath is always with you, serving as the key to self-awareness and remembrance of your choices. In stressful circumstances it is easy to forget that while circumstances change, there is a changeless and peaceful place within you—the Inner Self—that remains capable of observing the constant movies of the mind without becoming completely identified with them.

(c) Breathe in and let your breath travel all the way out. The next breath comes automatically, and the diaphragm resets. Count down, ten to one or five to one, or remember *Ham Sah* (I am the self that observes). The frequent use of such mini-relaxation responses throughout the day helps to reinforce the sense of control and choice.

2. **Optimal health is the product of both physical and mental factors.**

Goals to work for include:

(a) Exercise for at least twenty minutes, a minimum of three days a week. Depending on your physical condition, this can be aerobic or stretching exercise. The yoga exercises can be done as a block or a few at a time, several times daily.

(b) Eat consciously. Allow your bodily needs to regulate your diet rather than being a slave to your immediate frame of mind. For most people, unless your physician has prescribed a special diet, guidelines include:

- Low or no caffeine
- Low sugar—sugar releases insulin and increases appetite, leading to further "unconscious eating" (intake not regulated by your body's true needs).
- Low fat—fat adds excess calories and increases the risk for heart disease and many forms of cancer. Cut down on fatty meat, pastries, cheese, and full-fat dairy products.
- High fiber—lots of fresh fruits, vegetables, and whole grains increase the movement of food residue through the digestive tract, lower cholesterol levels, and fill you up, resulting in reduced appetite and weight loss. They are also a source of vitamins, including the important antioxidant vitamins, A, C, and E, which help the body to neutralize many cancer-causing chemicals.

(c) Meditate daily. Practice yields both physiological and psychological benefits. It's important to maintain continuity in any practice, or it gradually fades out. If you don't have ten or twenty minutes for a meditation, take five. Five often stretches to ten and helps you to make progress in the continual deepening of your sense of inner peace. Regular practice is the cornerstone on which mini-relaxation response breaks are built. Since they are conditioned responses, the stronger the association between breathing and concentration built in long practices, the more effective short meditations and single breaths become.

3. You could think of yourself as healthy.

I am reminded of the former Olympic medalist, skier Jimmy Huega, whose promising career was prematurely terminated by multiple sclerosis (MS). After sinking into a debilitating depression, he realized that he had a choice. He could be a healthy person with MS or an unhealthy person with MS.

He began a program of regular physical exercise (which varies with his daily energy level and the course of his MS), proper nutrition, and meditation. His view of himself is as a superiorly healthy person who also has MS. What is your view of yourself? Is inner peace completely dependent on bodily condition?

4. Things change. Change is the only constant in life.
If you have commitment—a sense of looking for life's meaning—change is received with curiosity and openness rather than with fear and doubt. If you feel resistant to change, try letting go and looking within. Remember "don't know"? Allowing yourself to be confused allows your mind to remain open to possibilities. Trying to control the world by insisting that you know can be a potent prescription for suffering and a real limit to experiencing "newness."

5. Your beliefs are incredibly powerful.
Consider the following experiment. Women with morning sickness were asked to swallow intragastric balloons as an objective measure of their stomach contractions and associated nausea. They were then told that they would receive a powerful antinausea drug. Instead, they were given syrup of ipecac, a powerful drug used to induce vomiting in cases of poisoning. Most of the women reported reduced nausea and had fewer stomach contractions. The power of their belief was stronger than the drug! Listen to what your mind tells you throughout the day and during your meditations. See what beliefs you hold and how strongly they can influence your perception of the world and of your health. Stay conscious of yourself.

6. The only escape from stress, fear, and doubt is to confront them directly and see them for what they are.
Attempts to hide from stress can only have brief apparent effectiveness. In actuality, hiding strengthens the original

fear and fuels the sense of helplessness and inability to cope. Attempts to avoid stress through drugs, alcohol, or repression weaken self-esteem. Repression is a mind/body mine field. Becoming unconscious of anything renders you blind and out of control, leading to mental and physical explosions which seem to have no basis since you have chosen not to look. Fears that are faced, even if the act is difficult, lead to transformation of attitudes, leaving you with an increased sense of self-worth, control, and inner strength. Sometimes it takes the help of others to confront these "dragons in the cellar." Don't be afraid to ask for help.

7. **Emotions fall into two broad categories, fear and love.**
Perhaps you remember the exercise in which anger, fear, and resentment were experienced in contrast to doing something well, loving or being loved, and experiencing humor. The fear category was associated with defense of the body—muscle tension, rapid heart beat, and a sense of holding tight. The love category was associated with openness and a sense of letting go and relaxation. Remember to pay attention to what state your body is in—then check your state of mind. Learning to let go is central to reducing stress and going beyond stress to peace of mind.

8. **Would you rather be right or would you rather experience peace?**
Ponder during your daily activities and interactions how much energy is used up in defending various positions that make you feel "right," worthy, okay. When you begin to realize your own precious, unique self-worth, the need to defend yourself will diminish, and your body will naturally relax.

9. **Accept yourself as you are.**
(Fat thighs, big noses, mistakes, health concerns, back pain, or other physical limitations notwithstanding.) This means

more than a grudging realization that you'll never again be some way that you used to be or some way that you wish to be. Acceptance means actually honoring yourself as you are now. To the extent that you can honor your Inner Self, which, unlike your body or mental capacities, never changes, you become free. This allows you to stop judging yourself negatively, which invariably brings forth feelings of blame, shame, guilt, or fear and escalates the cycle of anxiety and tension.

10. Practice forgiveness (letting go).

See people for who they are instead of who you want them to be. Then accept them as they are rather than judging them for who they're not. The more accepting you become of yourself, the more you can see others in the same light. The core of every human being is the same—unconditioned consciousness—the Self. See the Self in others. If you are religious or spiritual, you can think in terms of seeing the divine in one another. Remember the Sanskrit word *Namaste*? (My Self salutes your Self.)

11. Stay open to life's teachings.

There is an old aphorism that when the student is ready, the teacher will appear. The teacher may not come in easily recognizable garb. Sometimes the people who are peskiest or most difficult are the best teachers of patience, forgiveness, and self-respect. Do you remember the story of the petty tyrant?

12. Be patient. Patience means mindful awareness.

The usual understanding of patience is really impatience pushed to the breaking point. Patience is actually mindful attention to life—letting go of the expectations that pull the mind into the past or the future—so that you can remain in the moment without judging or blaming. When you feel impatient, notice it and take a breath of letting go, coming back to the central point of the observer, the Witness that notices without getting carried away by past conditioning. *Practice mindfulness.* Each day remember to do some activity with full attention. This trains your capacity to be mindful in every circumstance.

Whether the above attitudes and practices seem close at hand or very far from where you are, they can be realized by anyone who is truly motivated to become free from past conditioning. These goals are not realized in the reading of one book or many. They are a process of gradual unfolding— a gentle awakening rather than a storming of the citadel by force. Like anything of value, self-awareness grows best when nurtured with respect and attention. It's human nature for attention to wander and to seemingly forget things that have been learned. Yet, since all these learnings are stored within the mind, and since new learnings spring from the Self, they can never be completely forgotten. Changes in attitude and understanding may come forward at any time and in ways that surprise and delight you. Be assured that the efforts you have already made will continue to enrich you. Keep your heart and mind on the goal, and go easy with yourself along the way. The goal is closer than you might think.

> My inside, listen to me, the greatest spirit,
> the Teacher, is near,
> wake up, wake up!
> Run to his feet—
> he is standing close to your head right now.
> You have slept for millions and millions of years.
> Why not wake up this morning?
>
> —*Kabir*
> *version by Robert Bly*

Additional Reading

Meditation

Benson, Herbert, and Miriam Z. Klipper. *The Relaxation Response*. New York, Avon Books, 1976.

———, and William Proctor. *Beyond the Relaxation Response*. New York, Berkley, 1985.

Dhiravamsa. *The Dynamic Way of Meditation*. North Hollywood, CA, Newcastle, 1983.

Golas, Thaddeus. *The Lazy Man's Guide to Enlightenment*. Redway, CA, Seed Center, 1972.

Goldstein, Joseph. *The Experience of Insight: A Simple and Direct Guide to Buddhist Meditation*. Boston, Shambhala Publications, 1983.

Hanh, Thich N. *The Miracle of Mindfulness! A Manual on Meditation*. Boston, Beacon Press, 1976.

Kaplan, Aryeh. *Jewish Meditation: A Practical Guide*. New York, Schocken Books, 1985.

LeShan, Lawrence. *How To Meditate*. New York, Bantam Books, 1974.

Levine, Stephen. *A Gradual Awakening*. New York, Anchor Books, 1979.

Muktananda, Swami. *Meditate*. Albany, State University of New York Press, 1980.

Pennington, M. Basil. *Centering Prayer: Renewing an Ancient Christian Prayer Form*. New York, Image Books, 1982.

Ram Dass. *Journey of Awakening: A Meditator's Guidebook*. New York, Bantam Books, 1978.

Suzuki, Shunryu. *Zen Mind Beginner's Mind*. New York, John Weatherhill, 1970.

Stretching and Yoga

Carr, Rachel. *Be a Frog, a Bird or a Tree: Rachel Carr's Creative Yoga Exercises for Children*. New York, Doubleday, 1973.

———. *Yoga for All Ages*. New York, Simon & Shuster, 1972.

Christensen, Alice, and David Rankin. *Easy Does It Yoga: Yoga for Older People*. New York, Harper & Row, 1979.

Dechanet, J. M. *Christian Yoga*. New York, Perennial Library, 1956.

Hittleman, Richard. *Yoga: 28 Day Exercise Plan*. New York, Bantam Books, 1973.

Iyengar, B. K. S. *The Concise Light on Yoga*. New York, Schocken Books, 1982.

Lidell, Lucy, with Narayani and Giris Rabinovitch. *The Sivananda Companion to Yoga*. New York, Simon & Schuster, 1983.

Mandrell, Prema, and Sarala Troy. *Hatha Yoga for Meditators*. South Fallsburg, NY, SYDA Foundation, 1985.

Satchitananda, Yogiraj Sri Swami. *Integral Yoga Hatha*. New York, Holt, Rinehart & Winston, 1975.

Vishnudevananda, Swami. *The Complete Illustrated Book of Yoga*. New York, Pocket Books, 1981.

Popular Science and Medicine

Benson, Herbert. *The Mind/Body Effect*. New York, Simon & Schuster, 1979.

Bohm, David. *Wholeness and the Implicate Order*. Boston, Ark Paperbacks, 1980.

Capra, Fritjof. *The Tao of Physics*. New York, Bantam Books, 1977.

Cousins, Norman. *Anatomy of an Illness*. New York, W.W. Norton, 1979.

Dossey, Larry. *Space, Time and Medicine*. Boston, Shambhala Publications, 1982.

Eisenberg, David, with Thomas Lee Wright. *Encounters with Qi: Exploring Chinese Medicine*. New York, W.W. Norton, 1985.

Gillespie, Peggy Roggenbuck, and Lynn Bechtel. *Less Stress in 30 Days*. New York, Plume Books, 1986.

Locke, Steven, and Douglas Colligan. *The Healer Within: The New Medicine of Mind and Body*. New York, E.P. Dutton, 1986.

Pelletier, Kenneth. *Longevity: Fulfilling Our Biological Potential*. New York, Dell Books, 1982.

————. *Mind as Healer, Mind as Slayer*. New York, Dell Books, 1977.

Seligman, Martin E. P. *Helplessness: On Depression, Development and Death*. New York, W.H. Freeman & Co., 1975.

Siegel, Bernie S. *Love, Medicine and Miracles*. New York, Harper & Row, 1986.

Weil, Andrew. *Health and Healing: Understanding Conventional and Alternative Medicine*. Boston, Houghton Mifflin, 1983.

Yogananda, Paramahansa. *Autobiography of a Yogi*. Los Angeles, Self-Realization Fellowship, 1974.

Zukov, Gary. *The Dancing Wu Li Masters: An Overview of the New Physics.* New York, Bantam Books, 1979.

Psychology and Philosophy

Aranya, Swami Hariharananda. *Yoga Philosophy of Patanjali.* Albany, State University of New York Press, 1963.

Blanchard, Kenneth, and Spencer Johnson. *The One Minute Manager.* New York, Berkley, 1982.

Fields, Rick, with Peggy Taylor, Rex Weyler and Rick Ingrasci. *Chop Wood, Carry Water: A Guide to Finding Spiritual Fulfillment in Everyday Life.* Los Angeles, Jeremy P. Tarcher, 1984.

Foundation for Inner Peace. *A Course in Miracles.* Text, workbook, and workbook for teachers. Farmingdale, NY, Foundation for Inner Peace, 1975.

Frankl, Viktor. *Man's Search for Meaning.* New York, Washington Square Press, 1959.

Jampolsky, Gerald, M.D. *Love Is Letting Go of Fear.* Berkeley, CA, Celestial Arts, 1979.

———. *Teach Only Love: The Seven Principles of Attitudinal Healing.* New York, Bantam Books, 1983.

Kapleau, Phillip. *Three Pillars of Zen.* New York, Anchor Books, 1980.

Kushner, Harold S. *When Bad Things Happen to Good People.* New York, Schocken Books, 1981.

Levine, Stephen. *Meetings at the Edge: Conversations with the Grieving and the Dying, the Healing and the Healed.* New York, Doubleday, 1984.

———. *Who Dies: An Investigation of Conscious Living and Dying.* New York, Doubleday, 1982.

Peck, M. Scott. *The Road Less Traveled.* New York, Touchstone, 1978.

Prather, Hugh. *Notes on Love and Courage.* New York, Doubleday, 1977.

———. *Notes to Myself.* New York, Bantam Books, 1970.

Ring, Kenneth. *Heading Toward Omega: In Search of the Meaning of the Near-death Experience.* New York, William Morrow & Co., 1984.

Wilber, Ken. *No Boundary.* Boston, New Science Library, 1981.

Reframing and Creative Imagination

Achterberg, Jeanne. *Imagery in Healing: Shamanism and Modern Medicine.* Boston, New Science Library, 1985.

Bry, Adelaide, and Marjorie Bair. *Directing the Movies of the Mind: Visualization for Health and Insight.* New York, Harper & Row, 1978.

Edwards, Betty. *Drawing on the Right Side of the Brain*. Los Angeles, Jeremy P. Tarcher, 1979.

Gawain, Shakti. *Creative Visualization*. New York, Bantam Books, 1979.

Matthews-Simonton, Stephanie, O. Carl Simonton, and James L. Creighton. *Getting Well Again*. New York, Bantam Books, 1978.

Peseschkian, Nossrat. *Oriental Stories as Tools in Psychotherapy*. New York, Springer-Verlag, 1979.

Rosen, Sidney. *My Voice Will Go With You: The Teaching Tales of Milton H. Erikson, M.D.* New York, W.W. Norton, 1982.

von Oech, Roger. *A Whack on the Side of the Head: How to Unlock Your Mind for Innovation*. New York, Warner Books, 1983.

Fiction

Bly, Robert. *The Kabir Book: Forty-four of the Ecstatic Poems of Kabir*. Boston, Beacon Press, 1971.

Caldwell, Taylor. *Dear and Glorious Physician*. New York, Bantam Books, 1959.

Castaneda, Carlos. *The Eagle's Gift*. New York, Pocket Books, 1981.

———. *The Fire from Within*. New York, Pocket Books, 1985.

———. *Journey to Ixtlan*. New York, Pocket Books, 1972.

———. *The Second Ring of Power*. New York, Pocket Books, 1977.

———. *A Separate Reality: Further Conversations with Don Juan*. New York, Pocket Books, 1971.

———. *Tales of Power*. New York, Pocket Books, 1974.

———. *The Teaching of Don Juan: A Yacqui Way of Knowledge*. New York, Pocket Books, 1972.

Heinlein, Robert A. *Stranger in a Strange Land*. New York, Berkley, 1968.

Hesse, Hermann. *Siddhartha*. New York, Bantam Books, 1983.

Self Assessment

Patients entering the Mind/Body Program are asked to obtain a letter of referral from their physicians first so that we can be sure that their medical symptoms have been properly assessed and treated insofar as possible. If a patient has no physician, we refer him or her to a hospital physician for an examination before entering the program. *Likewise, it is important for you to make sure that any physical symptoms you are experiencing have been properly evaluated before trying any self-help approaches.* Then you can rest assured that no helpful medical treatment has been overlooked.

Before the evaluation visit, each patient is mailed a comprehensive questionnaire concerning lifestyle (exercise and relaxation habits, social support, history of cigarette, alcohol, and caffeine use, weight and stress levels), medical symptoms, and a comprehensive psychological evaluation. The patients often learn a lot about themselves through filling out the questionnaires, and their answers guide the interview, helping us to know what other approaches, in addition to the Mind/Body Group, may be helpful. For instance, some patients are referred for psychotherapy concomitant with beginning the Mind/Body Group, or specifically to a psychiatrist who may prescribe medication that alleviates severe symptoms enough so that they can get more from the Mind/Body Group. Others may profit from entrance into an indepth yoga program or even by the suggestion of a specific book.

As you fill out the following questionnaires, the goals will be different since they may not be followed by an interview with a health-care provider or psychotherapist who can help put them into perspective. Should you feel that you need help, based on your awareness of yourself through completing these questionnaires, seek professional assistance. Clearly, no book or questionnaire can determine your symptoms or provide treatment. At best they are rough guides.

The purpose of this self-assessment is twofold:

- To increase your awareness of your physical state, and the thoughts, emotions, and behaviors that interact with it.
- To allow you to evaluate yourself *now*, before you begin to learn and apply the tools and attitudes provided by this book, and *later*, after you feel comfortable using them. For this reason, the self-assessment forms are printed twice, once as a pre-evaluation and once as a post-evaluation.

The first questionnaire asks about physical symptoms you may experience, their frequency, intensity, and to what degree they interfere with your life. In many cases a physical symptom may not disappear, but it may become less frequent or bothersome.

The second questionnaire asks about thoughts, emotions, and behaviors that can distress people. Your score will reflect how you currently feel, but only you know if those feelings are typical of you and not your reaction to some stressful event that is happening now and may change shortly. It is best to fill out these questionnaires at a time that you feel is "typical" of your life so that they can be used to their best advantage. Wait a while if you are undergoing an unusually stressful period.

PRE-EVALUATION
MEDICAL SYMPTOMS CHECKLIST

Please read the following instructions carefully.
What follows is a list of medical symptoms that people sometimes have. Please indicate:

(A) How frequently you have the symptom, *if at all.* Circle a number on a scale of 0 to 7.

(B) The degree of discomfort caused by each symptom you have. Select a number on a scale of 0 to 10.

(C) The degree of interference caused by each symptom you have, that is, how much it interferes with your daily activities. Select a number on a scale of 0 to 10.

For each symptom that you *do have,* be sure to indicate all three responses.

SYMPTOMS	(A) FREQUENCY								(B) DEGREE OF DISCOMFORT 0 = None to 10 = Extreme	(C) DEGREE OF INTERFERENCE 0 = None to 10 = Extreme
	Never or almost never	Less than once a month	Once to twice a month	About once a week	2 to 3 times a week	4 to 6 times a week	Once a day	More than once a day		
1. Headache	0	1	2	3	4	5	6	7		
2. Visual symptoms (e.g., blurred or double vision)	0	1	2	3	4	5	6	7		
3. Dizziness or feeling faint	0	1	2	3	4	5	6	7		
4. Numbness	0	1	2	3	4	5	6	7		

SYMPTOMS	(A) FREQUENCY								(B) DEGREE OF DISCOMFORT 0 = None to 10 = Extreme	(C) DEGREE OF INTERFERENCE 0 = None to 10 = Extreme
	Never or almost never	Less than once a month	Once to twice a month	About once a week	2 to 3 times a week	4 to 6 times a week	Once a day	More than once a day		
5. Ringing in the ears	0	1	2	3	4	5	6	7		
6. Nausea	0	1	2	3	4	5	6	7		
7. Vomiting	0	1	2	3	4	5	6	7		
8. Constipation	0	1	2	3	4	5	6	7		
9. Loose stools	0	1	2	3	4	5	6	7		
10. Discomfort with urination (e.g., pressure, burning)	0	1	2	3	4	5	6	7		
11. Abdominal or stomach discomfort (e.g., pressure, burning, cramping) not related to menstruation	0	1	2	3	4	5	6	7		
12. Aching muscles	0	1	2	3	4	5	6	7		
13. Aching joints	0	1	2	3	4	5	6	7		

	0	1	2	3	4	5	6	7
14. Aching back	0	1	2	3	4	5	6	7
15. Discomfort in limb(s) (e.g., burning, aching)	0	1	2	3	4	5	6	7
16. Chest pain (e.g., burning, pressure, tightness)	0	1	2	3	4	5	6	7
17. Palpitations	0	1	2	3	4	5	6	7
18. Excessive sweating	0	1	2	3	4	5	6	7
19. Shortness of breath	0	1	2	3	4	5	6	7
20. Coughing	0	1	2	3	4	5	6	7
21. Wheezing	0	1	2	3	4	5	6	7
22. Skin problems (e.g., rash, itching)	0	1	2	3	4	5	6	7
23. Teeth grinding	0	1	2	3	4	5	6	7
24. Sleeping difficulties	0	1	2	3	4	5	6	7
25. Fatigue	0	1	2	3	4	5	6	7
26. Other:	0	1	2	3	4	5	6	7
	0	1	2	3	4	5	6	7
	0	1	2	3	4	5	6	7

(continued on next page)

WOMEN ONLY

	(A) FREQUENCY								(B) DEGREE OF DISCOMFORT 0 = None to 10 = Extreme	(C) DEGREE OF INTERFERENCE 0 = None to 10 = Extreme
	Never or almost never	Less than once a month	Once to twice a month	About once a week	2 to 3 times a week	4 to 6 times a week	Once a day	More than once a day		
1. Vaginal infection or irritation	0	1	2	3	4	5	6	7		
2. Menstrual irregularities	0	1	2	3	4	5	6	7		
3. Menstrual pain	0	1	2	3	4	5	6	7		
4. Premenstrual tension	0	1	2	3	4	5	6	7		
5. Premenstrual pain	0	1	2	3	4	5	6	7		

Copyright © Jane Leserman, Ph.D., and Claudia Dorrington, 1986.

PRE-EVALUATION
PSYCHOLOGICAL SYMPTOMS CHECKLIST

Circle the number, from 0 (never) to 4 (frequently), that represents the degree to which the following thoughts, feelings, and behaviors have bothered you during the past month.

THOUGHTS	BOTHERED				
	Never	Rarely	Sometimes	Often	Frequently
1. Awfulizing (taking things to their worst possible outcome)	0	1	2	3	4
2. Blaming myself	0	1	2	3	4
3. Blaming others	0	1	2	3	4
4. Difficulty concentrating	0	1	2	3	4
5. Holding grudges	0	1	2	3	4
6. Thinking and rethinking the same situation	0	1	2	3	4
7. Wishing I could "turn my mind off"	0	1	2	3	4
8. Constantly criticizing other people or situations	0	1	2	3	4
9. Worrying	0	1	2	3	4
10. Thinking something is wrong with my mind	0	1	2	3	4
11. Needing to be right	0	1	2	3	4
12. Feeling out of control	0	1	2	3	4

EMOTIONS					
1. Afraid of specific places or circumstances	0	1	2	3	4
2. Feeling like a victim	0	1	2	3	4
3. Anxious	0	1	2	3	4
4. Blue	0	1	2	3	4
5. Lonely	0	1	2	3	4

	BOTHERED				
EMOTIONS	Never	Rarely	Sometimes	Often	Frequently
6. Irritable	0	1	2	3	4
7. Wanting to throw things or hit people	0	1	2	3	4
8. Guilty	0	1	2	3	4
9. Feeling unfriendly	0	1	2	3	4
10. Uptight	0	1	2	3	4
11. Hopeless about the future	0	1	2	3	4
12. Wanting to "pull the covers over my head"	0	1	2	3	4
13. Feeling that other people don't like me	0	1	2	3	4
14. Upset over criticism	0	1	2	3	4

BEHAVIORS

1. Nail or cuticle biting	0	1	2	3	4
2. Using tobacco in any form	0	1	2	3	4
3. Taking tranquilizers or "street" drugs to change mood	0	1	2	3	4
4. Drinking alcoholic beverages	0	1	2	3	4
5. Chewing gum or sucking candies	0	1	2	3	4
6. Talking a lot	0	1	2	3	4
7. Crying a lot	0	1	2	3	4
8. Sleeping problems (too much or too little)	0	1	2	3	4
9. Eating problems (too much or too little)	0	1	2	3	4
10. Trouble communicating	0	1	2	3	4
11. Avoiding responsibilities	0	1	2	3	4
12. Too much caffeine	0	1	2	3	4

Evaluating the Results

Medical Symptoms Checklist

There is a big difference between having a symptom that interferes with your life and one that you can live with. In reviewing what symptoms bother you the most, pay close attention to interference. When you take the test again later, compare each symptom that you have reported on all dimensions—frequency, severity, and degree of interference with your life. *When in doubt, always consult a physician*.

Psychological Symptoms Checklist

Everyone experiences some of these symptoms, to various degrees, part of the time. But, if you find that many of your responses are in the *often* or *frequently* column (3 or 4), then you are experiencing significant distress and should consider discussing your feelings with a psychotherapist (psychologist, psychiatrist, or social worker specifically trained in psychological counseling). Self-help programs are no substitute for medication when indicated, or individual therapy, but can be very helpful adjuncts to either.

Compare the intensity of your symptoms on the first round with their intensity when you take the test again later. If you feel that your symptoms were bothersome enough that you were hoping for improvement that is not apparent, again you may wish to consider professional help.

I have noticed that many of our patients are at first reluctant to seek psychotherapy. They have misconceptions, thinking that only "crazy" people need such help. The truth is that almost every person can profit from psychotherapy. It is a way of learning to be free from past conditioning. Those who choose to go are usually "saner" than the rest of us. All psychologists must themselves receive psychotherapy so that they don't superimpose their own biases on their patients. I can attest to the value of my own therapy and hope that you will also keep an open mind toward it.

POST-EVALUATION
MEDICAL SYMPTOMS CHECKLIST

Please read the following instructions carefully. What follows is a list of medical symptoms that people sometimes have. Please indicate:

(A) How frequently you have the symptom, *if at all*. Circle a number on a scale of 0 to 7.

(B) The degree of discomfort caused by each symptom you have. Select a number on a scale of 0 to 10.

(C) The degree of interference caused by each symptom you have, that is, how much it interferes with your daily activities. Select a number on a scale of 0 to 10.

For each symptom that you *do have*, be sure to indicate all three responses.

SYMPTOMS	(A) FREQUENCY — Never or almost never	Less than once a month	Once to twice a month	About once a week	2 to 3 times a week	4 to 6 times a week	Once a day	More than once a day	(B) DEGREE OF DISCOMFORT 0 = None to 10 = Extreme	(C) DEGREE OF INTERFERENCE 0 = None to 10 = Extreme
1. Headache	0	1	2	3	4	5	6	7		
2. Visual symptoms (e.g., blurred or double vision)	0	1	2	3	4	5	6	7		
3. Dizziness or feeling faint	0	1	2	3	4	5	6	7		
4. Numbness	0	1	2	3	4	5	6	7		

SYMPTOMS	(A) FREQUENCY								(B) DEGREE OF DISCOMFORT	(C) DEGREE OF INTERFERENCE
	Never or almost never	Less than once a month	Once to twice a month	About once a week	2 to 3 times a week	4 to 6 times a week	Once a day	More than once a day	0 = None to 10 = Extreme	0 = None to 10 = Extreme
5. Ringing in the ears	0	1	2	3	4	5	6	7		
6. Nausea	0	1	2	3	4	5	6	7		
7. Vomiting	0	1	2	3	4	5	6	7		
8. Constipation	0	1	2	3	4	5	6	7		
9. Loose stools	0	1	2	3	4	5	6	7		
10. Discomfort with urination (e.g., pressure, burning)	0	1	2	3	4	5	6	7		
11. Abdominal or stomach discomfort (e.g., pressure, burning, cramping) not related to menstruation	0	1	2	3	4	5	6	7		
12. Aching muscles	0	1	2	3	4	5	6	7		
13. Aching joints	0	1	2	3	4	5	6	7		

14. Aching back	0	1	2	3	4	5	6	7
15. Discomfort in limb(s) (e.g., burning, aching)	0	1	2	3	4	5	6	7
16. Chest pain (e.g., burning, pressure, tightness)	0	1	2	3	4	5	6	7
17. Palpitations	0	1	2	3	4	5	6	7
18. Excessive sweating	0	1	2	3	4	5	6	7
19. Shortness of breath	0	1	2	3	4	5	6	7
20. Coughing	0	1	2	3	4	5	6	7
21. Wheezing	0	1	2	3	4	5	6	7
22. Skin problems (e.g., rash, itching)	0	1	2	3	4	5	6	7
23. Teeth grinding	0	1	2	3	4	5	6	7
24. Sleeping difficulties	0	1	2	3	4	5	6	7
25. Fatigue	0	1	2	3	4	5	6	7
26. Other:	0	1	2	3	4	5	6	7
	0	1	2	3	4	5	6	7

(continued on next page)

WOMEN ONLY	(A) FREQUENCY								(B) DEGREE OF DISCOMFORT	(C) DEGREE OF INTERFERENCE
	Never or almost never	Less than once a month	Once to twice a month	About once a week	2 to 3 times a week	4 to 6 times a week	Once a day	More than once a day	0 = None to 10 = Extreme	0 = None to 10 = Extreme
1. Vaginal infection or irritation	0	1	2	3	4	5	6	7		
2. Menstrual irregularities	0	1	2	3	4	5	6	7		
3. Menstrual pain	0	1	2	3	4	5	6	7		
4. Premenstrual tension	0	1	2	3	4	5	6	7		
5. Premenstrual pain	0	1	2	3	4	5	6	7		

POST-EVALUATION
PSYCHOLOGICAL SYMPTOMS CHECKLIST

Circle the number, from 0 (never) to 4 (frequently), that represents the degree to which the following thoughts, feelings, and behaviors have bothered you during the past month.

THOUGHTS	Never	Rarely	Sometimes	Often	Frequently
1. Awfulizing (taking things to their worst possible outcome)	0	1	2	3	4
2. Blaming myself	0	1	2	3	4
3. Blaming others	0	1	2	3	4
4. Difficulty concentrating	0	1	2	3	4
5. Holding grudges	0	1	2	3	4
6. Thinking and rethinking the same situation	0	1	2	3	4
7. Wishing I could "turn my mind off"	0	1	2	3	4
8. Constantly criticizing other people or situations	0	1	2	3	4
9. Worrying	0	1	2	3	4
10. Thinking something is wrong with my mind	0	1	2	3	4
11. Needing to be right	0	1	2	3	4
12. Feeling out of control	0	1	2	3	4

EMOTIONS					
1. Afraid of specific places or circumstances	0	1	2	3	4
2. Feeling like a victim	0	1	2	3	4
3. Anxious	0	1	2	3	4
4. Blue	0	1	2	3	4
5. Lonely	0	1	2	3	4

	BOTHERED				
EMOTIONS	Never	Rarely	Sometimes	Often	Frequently
6. Irritable	0	1	2	3	4
7. Wanting to throw things or hit people	0	1	2	3	4
8. Guilty	0	1	2	3	4
9. Feeling unfriendly	0	1	2	3	4
10. Uptight	0	1	2	3	4
11. Hopeless about the future	0	1	2	3	4
12. Wanting to "pull the covers over my head"	0	1	2	3	4
13. Feeling that other people don't like me	0	1	2	3	4
14. Upset over criticism	0	1	2	3	4

BEHAVIORS					
1. Nail or cuticle biting	0	1	2	3	4
2. Using tobacco in any form	0	1	2	3	4
3. Taking tranquilizers or "street" drugs to change mood	0	1	2	3	4
4. Drinking alcoholic beverages	0	1	2	3	4
5. Chewing gum or sucking candies	0	1	2	3	4
6. Talking a lot	0	1	2	3	4
7. Crying a lot	0	1	2	3	4
8. Sleeping problems (too much or too little)	0	1	2	3	4
9. Eating problems (too much or too little)	0	1	2	3	4
10. Trouble communicating	0	1	2	3	4
11. Avoiding responsibilities	0	1	2	3	4
12. Too much caffeine	0	1	2	3	4

Index

NON-FICTION AVAILABLE FROM PATHWAY